GERANIUMS

Brenda Delamain and Dawn Kendall

GERANIUMS

Brenda Delamain and Dawn Kendall

CHRISTOPHER HELM
London

First Published 1987

Christopher Helm (Publishers) Ltd,
Imperial House, 21-25 North Street,
Bromley, Kent. BRI ISD

ISBN 0-7470-0604-0

Designed by Jaap Koster
Colour Separations and film work by
Bascands, Christchurch
Typeset by Saba Graphics Ltd
Christchurch
Printed by Kyodo-Shing Loong
Singapore

Acknowledgements

Thanks are due to the many people who allowed us to photograph their plants and provided information: to Ian Buchanan of the A.R.A. Botanical gradens, Bruce Jones, Nicholas Lodewyck, Mr and Mrs Manson, Phil and Gail Waterhouse, Ann Wilcox and the many other people who unknowingly provided decorated fences, not forgetting Telecom for floral poles.

My thanks, also, to Mary MacGregor for doing the floral art arrangements and Mrs N.J. van Berkel of Windhoek, Namibia, for her colour transparencies of Sarcocaulons.

Finally I am grateful for the expert advice of Graham Rice in England and Bev Farmer and Jean Llewwllyn in Australia. Particular thanks to Mr Michael ffolliott-Foster for the many hours spent sorting out my muddles and for editing this book.

Contents

Foreword

The increasing popularity of the geranium family will come as no surprise to the substantial number of enthusiastic growers of these attractive, versatile and resilient plants. Now gardeners with a much broader range of interests are aware that 'geranium' means far more than the regal and zonal pelargonium.

There was a time when 'geraniums' were amongst the most popular of pot and summer bedding plants. Then disease took its toll, only the more dedicated growers kept up their commitment and it wasn't until the arrival of excellent seed-raised strains that their fortunes revived amongst gardeners in general. Now the circle is turning again, the old varieties are being sought out and new ones are being bred. A National Collection has been set up at Fibrex Nurseries near Stratford on Avon.

But this enthusiasm amongst gardeners does no more than reflect the natural versatility of the group. For the family includes far more good garden plants than simply the much-loved 'geraniums'. There is everything from alpine plants to tender succulents, annuals to shrubs and although it is the regal and zonal pelargoniums which have the longest record of popularity, hardy perennial geraniums have a large and growing following and the smaller groups also have their devotees.

The defiant 'geranium' in its pot on the windowsill is familiar to even the most reluctant gardener who, when inspired by the ease which it can be cultivated more effectively, may well turn into a real fan. But there's no doubt that the rising stars are the hardy geraniums grown as ground cover plants, as rock plants or in shady borders. Their capacity for long flowering, combined with a cheerful tendency to flourish without pampering, endears them to most gardeners and they are sufficiently diverse for the average garden to host quite a collection. Even the smaller groups in the family such as the erodiums and sarcocaulons are now being collected by an increasing band of enthusiasts.

This book introduces them all to the relative newcomer while still providing insights for the wiser and more experienced enthusiast. The invaluable pictures make an excellent guide to the choice of varieties for expert and newcomer alike. I'm sure this book will help foster a greater enthusiasm for whole geranium family.

Graham Rice
Technical Consultant for *Practical Gardening*

Introduction

What is a geranium? That seems a ridiculous question – everybody knows: geraniums are those red flowers (occasionally pink or white) in pots or hanging baskets on window-sills or patios. They are known from one side of the world to the other: the brilliant splashes of red growing in the window-boxes of Switzerland, or tumbling from the urns of formal gardens in France; strikingly trained against the white walls and dark hedges of Spain; sitting in pots on the verandahs of Italy, or around the swimming pools of California. That blaze of scarlet on a thousand postcards of Buckingham Palace, vying with the colourful jackets of the guards – yes, geraniums. They bask in the sun of Sydney, falling in profusion down the sandstone walls of the city, and I have even seen a picture of a family in Siberia peering out of an ice-framed window with, between them on the window-sill as a contrast to that otherwise drab and colourless scene, a geranium in a pot with one pink blossom and a few green leaves. Indeed, my own earliest memory of geraniums also conjures up a window-sill – my childhood home in the industrial north-east of England and a warm, glowing, red patch against the grey of the sky and stone buildings.

Everybody knows what a geranium is – but have you ever met one of those knowing people who say, 'Very nice – but of course they are not really geraniums at all, are they?' and unfortunately, in a way, they are right. So – 'When is a geranium not a geranium?' – the answer – 'When it is a pelargonium.' Most garden 'geraniums' are, in fact, pelargoniums.

This book should correctly have been named *An Introduction to Geraniaceae*, then even knowing friends could not complain. However, the word geranium is so evocative of the cheerful, prolific plants that brighten our gardens and homes that I make no apology for using it as a general descriptive term for the whole Geraniaceae family (hereafter referred to as the Geranium family). After all both have their roots in the same Greek word, *Geranos*, a crane, and though the name geranium correctly refers to only one group of the family, it is now generally used for zonal and ivy-leaved pelargoniums as well.

The confusion between geraniums and pelargoniums arose in the late seventeenth and early eighteenth centuries, when Euro-pean botanists and gardeners were importing plants from all over the world for their orangeries and collections. From the Cape Colony (now South Africa) came an influx of plants obviously related to the crane's-bills or geraniums of Europe, all bearing the distinctive seed pods resembling the bill of a crane that so aptly led to the geranium's naming in the first place. It was only later, when botanists studied them in greater detail, that it was realized that the South African plants were, in fact, a slightly different genus. In 1789 they were named pelargoniums after the Greek word *Pelargos*, a stork. Just to add to the confusion, another branch of the family are called erodium after the word *Erodios*, a heron, although these are commonly known as storksbill. Provided you are a competent ornithologist you will be able to pick the difference in an instant. However, in case you are not – and in the interests of accuracy – they will all be differentiated in the final chapter. Sufficient, now, to say that the correct names will be used throughout the book. When a zonal pelargonium is mentioned it will be the plant usually called a geranium and, likewise, ivy-leaved pelargonium will refer to the spra-wling ivy geranium which is a common sight in gardens.

Names aside, geraniums and pelargoni-ums are both fun to collect and to grow. Perhaps one of the greatest pleasures they bring is that, given the right conditions, they will grow almost anywhere, and even given the wrong conditions they struggle on and make an effort. I was recently involved in helping to clear a neglected coastal garden; as we toiled through buffalo grass, gorse and second-growth bush, a flash of red shone up through the tangle of weeds and there it was, the one surviving flower, a zonal pelargonium. It had survived hard clay soil, salt winds, weeds, weather and insects – admittedly it was not a magnificent specimen but it was a fighter, it had survived and it had flowered.

Though much can be made of the gera-nium and pelargonium's ability to survive it must be said, at the same time, that they are still susceptible to disease and insect depredation – to grow them to their full glory they need just as much care as roses or lilies.

One of the simplest of plants to propagate, both from cuttings and seed; easy to hybridize, and providing an infinite variety for the collector, they will provide ample rewards for care and attention. It is to be hoped that within the limiting confines of this *Introduction to Geraniums*, there will be sufficient information to stimulate an interest in these heart-warming and colourful plants and to enable them to be grown to the best possible advantage.

In Europe and America, pelargoniums are big business – produced in factories by their millions, and used extensively as bedding plants for public parks and as pot plants for the home and garden. In Australia, too, they provoke considerable interest, and hybridists there have produced many new and exciting cultivars. For some reason, though, they seem to have bypassed New Zealand; there is no Geranium Society and it is often hard to buy a named plant in shops; public places seem not to have beds of these eye-catching plants which provide months of colour through the late spring and summer. This situation may now be changing as there has been a recent upsurge of interest in 'geraniums', with a number of nurseries entirely devoted to these plants and to importing new cultivars each year. Seed firms are also beginning to import seed.

An awareness of the immense variety of plants in the Geranium family – from the magnificent regal pelargonium to the smallest rockery plant – is becoming steadily more apparent. There is variation not only in plant size, but also in leaf form and colour, with colours ranging from almost black to lime-green and gold. Differences notwithstanding, they are all of the same family: all give generously of scent, flowers or colour; and all share the dominant spirit of survival and gaiety.

Natural Distribution and Spread

The first written mention of geraniums is in a book of herbal remedies by Dioscorides, a Greek doctor who served with the Roman legions in the days of Nero. He called them geranions and he could have been referring to any one of a number of plants in the Geranium family that were native to Europe. The name, derived from *Geranos*, Greek for crane – or the English version 'crane's bill' – had probably existed for many centuries before that. The reason for the name is obvious when the seed pod is compared with the crane's beak.

It is now known that the family Geraniaceae contains 750 species spread throughout the temperate and subtropical regions of the world, but of particular abundance in South Africa which contains 90 per cent of the species. There are members of the family represented in the native flora of every continent – excluding Antarctica – and scattered over a wide range of islands including Madeira, St Helena and Tristan da Cunha in the Atlantic; the Australian continent, the Chatham Islands, Hawaii and New Zealand in the Pacific; and Madagascar in the Indian Ocean (Figure 1).

Early explorers and botanists, seeing the distinctive seed head, classified them all under the heading of Geraniaceae, but there are now five genera recognised: *Erodium, Geranium, Monsonia, Pelargonium* and *Sarcocaulon*. The similarities also extend to the flowers, which all have five petals and five sepals.

The early interest in plants being mainly for their medicinal properties, it is not surprising that, after Dioscorides, the next mention of the Geraniaceae is again in a text on herbs. John Gerard, in a book published in 1597, mentions the dove's-foot crane's-bill, *Geranium molle*, of the European countryside:

The herbe and roots, dried, beaten into moste fine powder, and given half a spoonful fasting, and the like quantitie to bedwards in red wine or claret for the space of one and twenty daies together cure miraculously ruptures and burstings, as myself have proved, whereby I have gotten crownes and credit. If the ruptures are in aged persons, the herbes should be mixed with the powder of nine red snailes (those without shels) dried in an oven.

Figure 1 The natural distribution of Geraniaceae

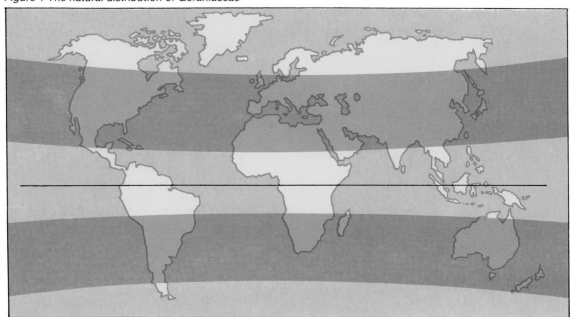

Other herbals advocated its use as a styptic (a substance that checks bleeding) and it was recommended for medicinal use in cases of internal bleeding.

While members of the Geranium family are not generally regarded to be food plants, other than the use of scented-leaved pelargoniums for flavouring, it is recorded by William Colenso, an early missionary in New Zealand, that the Maoris occasionally ate the roots of the native Australian and New Zealand species *G. australe*. This plant grew as a weed in their kumara (sweet potato) plots, they called it 'matua kumara' – father of the kumara. If the kumara crop failed the 'matua kumara' was allowed to grow and its slightly tuberous roots were eaten, but probably only in situations of dire necessity.

During the reign of Charles I, scented-leaved pelargoniums brought by sailors started to make their appearance in the country cottages and manor-houses of England. Other than decorative uses were soon found for these plants – bowls of pot pourri containing the scented geranium leaves were used to sweeten the musty odours which frequently prevailed in houses and cottages of that time; potted plants were probably used for the same purpose. Much later, during the Victorian era, it became quite a vogue to plant the scented-leaved pelargoniums along the edges of garden walks, or to set them in pots in such places as the corners of the stairs so that as the long skirts of the ladies brushed past, the scent was released – an early precursor to the air freshener.

Early in the seventeenth century, voyages made by the Dutch East India Company via the Cape of Good Hope resulted in South African plants being taken to Europe. Mention is made of *Pelargonium zonale* being sent by the governor of Cape Colony to Holland in 1609. Thomas Johnson, in 1633, describes a night-scented plant in the Lambeth gardens of John Tradescant (gardener to Queen Henrietta Maria, wife of Charles 1); he says, 'We may fitly call it sweet India storksbill or painted storksbill and, in Latin, *Geranium indicum odoratum flore maculats.*' Fortunately for gardeners writing labels, the latter name has not persisted and it is now known as *P. triste* (sad, or dull coloured).

By 1687, according to a Dutch catalogue, the number of Geraniaceae varieties in Europe had risen to ten and included *P. cucullatum* – father of the present regal pelargoniums. The principal parent of the many ivy-leaved cultivars, *P. peltatum,* was introduced to Holland in 1700. The earliest reference to *P. inquinans,* the main ancestor of the zonal pelargonium, states that it was seen in 1714 growing in the garden of Bishop Compton in England. It came originally from the banks of the Fish River in South Africa.

During the next two centuries, pelargoniums became increasingly popular and large numbers were to be found in the conservatories and greenhouses of the wealthy who, as befitted the times, were blessed with many gardeners. Much experimentation was undertaken and many hybrids were produced in a continued search for bigger, better and more vari-coloured blooms.

However, with the advent of two world wars, and the subsequent changes in economic climate and land ownership, the glasshouses of the hitherto wealthy were either abandoned or turned over to food production. In like manner, the quest for bigger and better pelargoniums became a casualty. It was not until some years after the second world war that, with the arrival of more stable conditions, an enthusiasm for these plants was revived. Geranium and pelargonium societies were established in many parts of the world and this led not only to the rediscovery of many time-honoured cultivars, but also – and most importantly – to efforts being made to sort out the muddle which generations of pelargonium growers had brought to the much vexed question of nomenclature.

The introduction of a standardised nomenclature made it possible not only to identify cultivars which had already been developed but also to classify new cultivars as they occur.

Natural Habitat and Adaptations

The pelargonium species from which the majority of the cultivated types are descended have one thing in common – they are able to grow in poor terrain, often stony or sandy, and in dry areas or where there are long periods of drought interspersed with heavy seasonal rains, and have readily naturalised in countries which duplicate these natural environments, for example of California, Australia and the Mediterranean region. The plants have evolved to deal with these hardships in many different ways, according to the area and circumstances in which they grow. In particular, the Geraniaceae family have set about obtaining and retaining water in several ways.

Most of the pelargoniums have succulent stems and fleshy leaves for storing water, some have developed tuberous roots for the same purpose, others have long fibrous roots – in South Africa *P. cucullatum* plants have been recorded with roots reaching a depth of more than 1.5 m (5 ft).

Just as some species have found ways of reaching and storing water, others have found methods of preventing its loss. Different forms of leaves have evolved to counter excessive evaporation, for example the hairy leaf of *P. tomentosum* or the fine thread-like foliage of *P. luridum* which reduces the surface area subject to evaporation.

While most species live in compact clumps in the full sun, a few shelter in the shade of other plants and grow long and straggly, reaching their leaves outward and upward to the available light.

The success of the pelargoniums in extracting the maximum available amount of water from their environment means that they are sometimes the only green herbage in an arid area and are therefore an open invitation to grazing animals. To counter this hazard, some species have developed hard spines of adapted stipules, others have an unpleasant acid taste, and yet others – and these are many – have strong scents. There are a large number of various scented species, such as the nutmeg-scented *P. fragrans,* the rose-scented *P. graveolens*, and an abundance of others which will be described in the final chapter.

The Sarcocaulon genus appears to require the least amount of water. Species of this genus live in areas of south-west Africa where there can be several years without any precipitation.

Leaf shape and colour are just as varied as scent (Figure 2). Colours range from white to deep purple-brown, through yellow and green, bronze and red, single coloured and multicoloured, patched and blotched, ringed, lined and veined. Leaf configuration

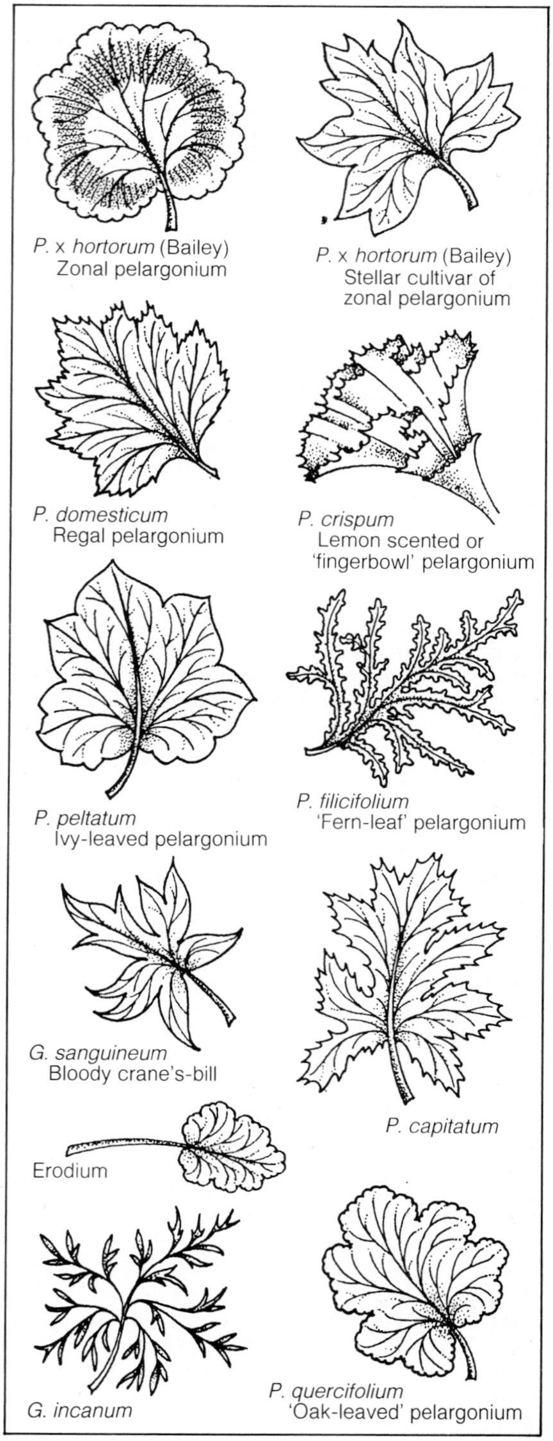

Figure 2 Leaf shapes

P. x *hortorum* (Bailey)
Zonal pelargonium

P. x *hortorum* (Bailey)
Stellar cultivar of
zonal pelargonium

P. *domesticum*
Regal pelargonium

P. *crispum*
Lemon scented or
'fingerbowl' pelargonium

P. *peltatum*
Ivy-leaved pelargonium

P. *filicifolium*
'Fern-leaf' pelargonium

G. *sanguineum*
Bloody crane's-bill

P. *capitatum*

Erodium

G. *incanum*

P. *quercifolium*
'Oak-leaved' pelargonium

is equally varied, ranging from the rounded shape of the zonal pelargoniums, to the ridged triangular shape of the regal pelargoniums or the ivy-leaved forms, or to a multiplicity of other patterns – some lobed, others deeply indented or serrated. It is not known what effect these variations have upon browsing animals; they may act merely as camouflage, or they may suggest unappetising or poisonous vegetation.

The ultimate test of a plant's adaptability, as with all living things, is whether it produces any offspring. The plant with successful offspring will determine the future genetic makeup of the species. Geraniaceae species propagate both by seed and by vegetative rooting. Naturally, the former is probably the commonest method, although where top-heavy or straggling pelargonium plants break or fall to the ground they often root readily. It is possible that wind and adherence to animal fur may also play a part in the breaking off and subsequent dispersal of cuttings. Broken pieces survive for many days on the water stored in their succulent stems, and are able to root as soon as they find a favourable medium.

In the Geranium family, the characteristic birds-bill seed pod is composed of five long carpels around a central axis, each with a seed attached. As each fruit reaches maturity, it dries and splits from the base upwards and each carpel twists, forming a spring, which ejects the seed from the plant.

The seed dispersal method is the easiest way to distinguish between the three main Geraniaceae genera (Figure 3).

In erodiums, the carpel forms a corkscrew-like tail with a right-angled awn which thrusts the seeds away so violently that they can travel some distance. When the seed lands on the ground, the awn holds the screw above the ground. With any increase in humidity the screw straightens – then coils again as it dries – this action screws the seed into the ground; barbs on the seed prevent any subsequent humidity change from screwing it out again. An ingenious example of natural engineering.

Pelargonium seeds are similar, but have the addition of thistledown-like fluff which enables them to become windborne.

Geranium carpels, instead of twisting spirally, curl upwards in a coil. As this coils and uncoils in a similar way to the erodium carpel, the seeds are separated from the carpel and catapulted away from the plant without any attachments.

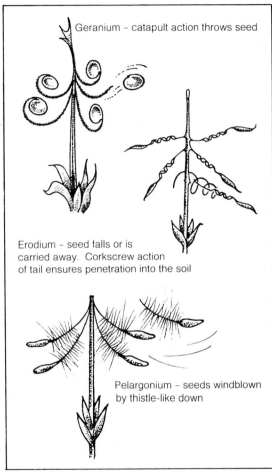

Figure 3 Seed dispersal of the Geraniaceae

Conditions for Cultivation

As a consequence of the many countries that provide the natural habitats of the Geraniaceae, there are suitable members of the family for most places in a garden or indoors.

Geraniums and erodiums are very variable in their choices of environment, some liking shady positions and heavy soils and others, an open sunny situation and light soils, depending on their place of origin.

There are, however, basic requirements that are common to all pelargoniums bearing in mind that the majority of the cultivated varieties have originated in South Africa.

- A light, gritty, well aerated soil mix that allows easy root penetration.
- A soil type with a neutral to slightly acid pH reaction and ample potassium, but not too much nitrogen.
- A position which has plenty of sun and warmth, with protection from strong winds and driving rain.
- Ample, free-draining water to the roots.
- Protection from heavy frosts or extremes of heat.
- Regular applications of light fertiliser during the flowering period, but not over feeding.
- Protection from disease and insects.

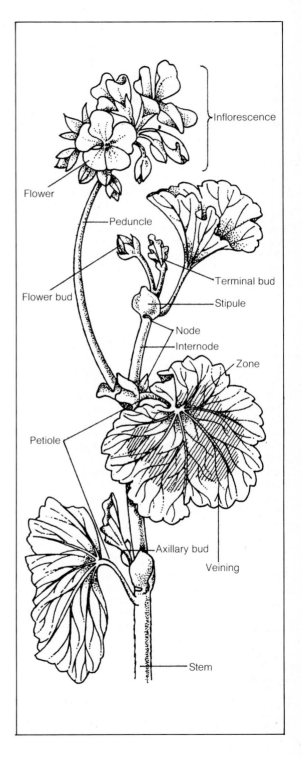

Figure 4 Names of parts

Every garden is different, only the gardener can find the best place for any particular plant. Often, the final choice results from trial and error – a position that seems eminently suitable may have perfect light and soil but poor drainage, or good drainage but too much shade or wind. The recommendations which follow, however, outline general environmental requirements.

Light

Pelargoniums are light lovers. They can endure early morning shade but are best suited to a position where they receive full sun for the greater part of the day. Light promotes compact growth and abundant flowering.

A plant deprived of light for any length of time will grow long limbed and lopsided, stretching towards the nearest light source. It will also produce less flowers and the colour of those that are produced will be faded.

A favourable planting position is along the wall of a house or building that faces into the sun, with protection from excessive wind and rain yet with ample light.

Plants in pots should also be placed where there is good light. If they are to be grown inside, they should be placed on a window-sill or as near to a window as possible. Even in a light, sunny room, if they do not have access to direct light, they will soon exhibit symptoms of light deprivation. They should be turned at least twice per week ensuring light to all sides of the plant.

At the same time, it must be noted that light through glass, particularly in the summertime, can be very intense. It can cause scorching and wilting of leaves through excessive transpiration. At such times it is preferable to move the plants outside. If this is not possible shade should be provided for part of the day and ample water and air circulation ensured.

Geraniums and erodiums, on the whole, prefer a mixture of sun and light shade.

Temperature

The natural habitat of pelargoniums is in sunny, temperate to subtropical climates with moderately even temperature for the greater part of the year but with slightly cooler winters. As many of the areas in which they are now grown can by no means be included in these climatic categories, it is sometimes necessary to simulate the required temperature conditions.

Optimum growing temperatures are from 7°C to 25°C (50°F to 77°F), with night temperatures several degrees lower than those of the daytime. However, they can tolerate a few degrees either side of the optimum for short periods. Where the temperature remains above 32°C (89°F) for several months, pelargoniums will not grow well, and in very cold areas they are best considered as glasshouse plants.

Although miniatures tend to be frost tender, most pelargoniums can survive in light frost. In frost-prone areas they fare best in positions where they are shaded in the early morning and are able to thaw out before the sun's rays reach them. It has also been observed that variegated-leaved varieties can endure slightly lower temperatures than the more customary green-leaved types.

If a heavy frost is predicted, it is advisable to cover outdoor plants with a plastic cover, or even newspaper, to give them some protection. In colder climates, during the winter, pelargoniums have to be brought inside. Where there are only occasional frosts an unheated glasshouse or frame is sufficient. However, where the temperatures frequently drop below freezing – especially in wet climates – heating is necessary, ideally at about 10°C to 15°C (55°F to 60°F). If regal pelargoniums are not kept below 15°C for approximately three months during the winter they will not form flower buds.

Geraniums and erodiums come from a wide variety of climates, generally, though not always, from cooler areas than pelargoniums. They can, subject to their areas of origin, stand frost or even snow, and may react badly to excessive heat. When buying new stock it is prudent to determine their natural habitats, if they are known, or to discuss their growth preferences with the nursery from which they have been bought. For instance, *G. anemonifolium* from the island of Madeira, or *G. atlanticum* from hot, dry banks in Spain and Morocco, would not thrive in the same conditions as *G. traversii* from the rather bleak shoreline of the Chatham Islands in the South Pacific, or *G. cinereum* from the mountain heights of the

Pyrenees. On the whole, however, geraniums are very tolerant plants which will endure a wider variation of temperatures than will pelargoniums.

Wind and Salt

Most Geraniaceae tolerate coastal positions and salt-laden atmospheres, though wind tolerance varies according to height. Low-growing geraniums and ivy-leaved pelargoniums are well situated to stand strong winds while zonal and regal pelargoniums are inclined to snap off, and flowers to shatter, if too exposed; for this reason they require shelter.

Water

Balanced watering is probably the most important factor in growing pelargoniums. In their native habitat, or when growing in open ground, they can endure quite lengthy periods without water. However, it is a different matter if they are being grown in pots. As their roots cannot reach downward and outward through large areas of soil to extract all the available moisture, it is important that adequate water is applied. Conversely, as their origin may often be associated with semi-arid conditions, too much water around the roots will cause rotting and the plant will die. The ideal is to keep the soil in the pot moist but not waterlogged.

A general rule of thumb is to water them twice a week in the summer, when heat, growth and transpiration are higher, and once a week during the winter. As with all 'general rules', exceptions will occur and these may be brought about by significant increases or decreases in temperature (the lower the temperature the less water is needed), light or atmospheric humidity. Differences in soil types or pot size also have a bearing on the amount of water required. A further 'general rule' is to soak the pots thoroughly and then repeat the process after the soil has nearly dried out. Another, and totally unscientific method, is to bury the finger into the potting mix: if the moisture level is at or below fingertip level more water is required.

More accurate scientific methods include the use of moisture meters or daily assessment of evapotranspiration levels by weighing the plant and the pot. Even the latest scientific papers on the subject admit that there are no simple rules regarding irrigation frequencies. The best basis is constant observation and experience.

A plant which has been deprived of sufficient water over a period of time will become woody and stunted in its growth, the leaves will be smaller with a dull olive-green appearance, and will often have an edging of dry tissue. First the stipules, then any forming flower buds will dry up and die. The remedy is to saturate the soil with water and increase future supply. Do not give any liquid fertiliser until the plant has developed a substantial amount of new foliage.

Symptoms of excess soil moisture and of short term lack of water are very similar – in both instances the leaves wilt and some develop yellow edges, the yellowing gradually covers the whole leaf. It is easy to determine which trouble afflicts the plant by studying the moisture level of the potting mix. Further evidence can be gained by examining the roots: those troubled by excess moisture will appear dark brown or black indicating that they have started to rot. Any valuable plants in this state can possibly be saved by cutting away all the damaged roots, pruning off two-thirds of the top foliage, repotting in fresh mix which is just moist to the touch and restricting the water supply for the next few weeks so that it is kept almost dry.

The watering method is also important. Plants growing in garden soil rarely need watering. If, however, watering does become necessary due to a period of extended drought, the preferred method would be to flood the soil around the plant, or plants, with a hose until it is thoroughly saturated. Sprinkle watering is not very effective as the large leaves deflect the water away from the roots where it is required. Surplus water on the flowers and leaves is also conducive to attacks of botrytis, which causes rotting of the flowers and leaf spot – this can often be seen in garden-grown plants after a period of heavy rain or high humidity.

Mist spraying can be used on small seedlings or small cuttings which do not have flowers or large leaves, but it is not recommended unless ventilation and air movement are good.

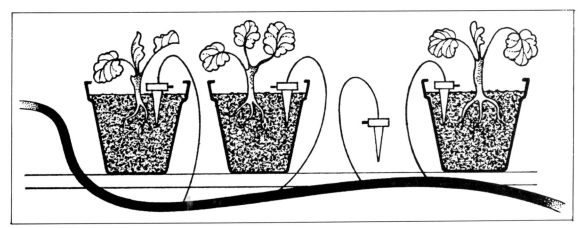

Watering of the soil surface in pots – with a hose or watering can – is a time-consuming method and is not always satisfactory. Care should be taken to see that the water is absorbed; sometimes when the mix is almost dry it is slow to re-absorb moisture and water runs down the walls of the pot and straight out of the drainage holes without moistening the soil. It is also possible to water the top half of the mix inadvertently while the lower half remains dry, this inhibits the development of a good root system.

The most effective way to water potted pelargoniums is to stand the whole pot in a container of water and allow the soil mix to suck the water up by capillary action until it is completely saturated. The pot should then be removed to drain; it should never be left standing in surplus water.

Commercial growers who have large numbers of pots to water – and who find it too arduous and expensive a task to move each pot – use capillary water matting or a plastic tubing irrigation system with fine tubing running to each pot from a central watering pipe. This system is used to give each plant a measured amount of water or liquid fertiliser (Figures 5 and 6).

Other small points to remember are that small pots will need more frequent watering than big ones; porous clay pots will require more frequent watering than plastic pots; and plants need less moisture during the winter months when temperature, growth and transpiration rates are lower.

Figure 5 Recently developed Multi-outlet Drippers (MOD), also known as spaghetti watering-systems, are very useful for controlled watering of large numbers of pots. Tubing (5 mm) carries water to regulating sticks which are plunged into individual pots. Each stick can be turned off, like a tap, if not required

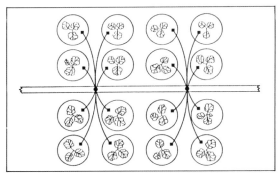

Figure 6 Eight pots can be watered from each MOD on a central pipe. The length of tubing can be altered to suit different situations

Soil

The main soil requirements of pelargoniums are good drainage, easy root run, moderate water holding capacity, a high volume of air space and neutral to slightly acid pH (6.5 – 7.0). The soil should also be substantial enough to support the roots of what can, sometimes, develop into a top-heavy plant. Freedom from toxins, pests and weed seeds is also desirable. Very high fertility soil is not suitable.

Pelargoniums will grow well in a clay-based soil, provided the ground has been dug deeply and mixed with coarse river sand, pulverised lava in the form of scoria or pumice grains, perlite or vermiculite to promote drainage and aeration. Some humus is also a desirable additive to assist with aeration.

Light sandy soils provide good drainage, however compost, peat moss, seaweed or any other humus source should be added to improve the nutritional status, assist with soil aeration and ensure adequate water retention. Easily compacted, fine sand may need the addition of gravel or scoria to help provide air space.

Very acid soils high in nitrogen and leaf mold or peat are not good situations for pelargoniums. However, such soils can be made usable by the addition of large quantities of coarse river sand, scoria, vermiculite or similar, to change their composition, and dolomite lime to bring them to the correct pH level. If available, clay loam should also be added.

Potting Mixes

Pelargoniums will grow in most commercial potting mixes as long as they are given the proper balance of water and fertiliser. Commercial mixes do, however, tend to be very light in weight and if used in plastic pots may not provide a sufficiently solid base for a large bushy plant. It is best to start cuttings and young plants in a light, sterile mix and then, when they have developed a good root system, to transfer them to a larger pot with a more substantial part-soil mix.

A standard potting compost, such as John Innes No 1, is a well-balanced mix for pelargoniums, however, many growers like to prepare their own potting mixes. These can vary according to the components that are available. The basic proportions are as follows:
- Heavy soil (clay loam)
  1 part soil, 2 parts organic matter, 2 parts coarse aggregate.
- Medium soil (loam, sandy clay loam)
  1 part soil, 1 part organic matter, 1 part coarse aggregate.
- Light soil (sandy loam)
  2 parts soil, 2 parts organic matter.

The organic matter is usually sphagnum moss peat as this is readily available, but compost or rotted organic manures can also be used. Coarse aggregates can be river sand, fine gravel, scoria, pumice, perlite or vermiculite.

To each bucketful of mix, one-third of a cup of dolomite lime and one-third of a cup of blood and bone, or one cup of commercial slow-release fertiliser, should be added.

After mixing, the consistency can be judged by squeezing a handful of moist mix – when released it should just break apart. If it falls apart into a crumbly mass it needs more soil, if it sticks together in a lump it needs more aggregate.

Granulated bark can be used instead of soil. Fine to medium potting-grade granulated bark, mixed with sand and a slow-release fertiliser, has been found to be suitable for pelargoniums.

Fertilisers

It has been claimed that pelargoniums do not require fertiliser but this has proved false. While they are not gross feeders, they respond as well to balanced feeding as any other plants. A very simplified explanation of the need for these nutrients is: 'nitrogen for leaf growth, phosphate for root growth and potassium for flowers.'

The N.P.K. values listed on the packets of most commercial fertilisers give the nitrogen, phosphate and potassium levels respectively of that particular mix. The ideal formula for pelargoniums is N.15 P.15 K.15, however, not many commercial fertiliser mixes have this formula. The one that is the nearest and has the lowest nitrogen level compared to the other elements should be used and applied at the lowest concentration level recommended on the packet.

The optimum soil chemical analysis for pelargoniums is:
   nitrogen 3.3 to 4.8% of dry matter
   phosphorous 0.40 to 0.67% of dry matter
   potassium 2.5 to 4.5% of dry matter
   calcium 0.81 to 1.2% of dry matter
   magnesium 0.20 to 0.52% of dry matter
   with trace elements

Soil testing is the only way to assess these levels accurately, but the average soil mix – as described in the previous section – should contain all these elements and, provided that a regular supply of fertiliser is given during the growing and flowering period, deficiencies should not occur.

Fertilisers can be administered through

slow-release pellets, fertigation or foliar feeding – all are satisfactory bearing in mind a few minor points:

- Slow-release pellets only last for four months. Scattering further pellets onto the soil surface is only effective where top watering is carried out. The four month supply, in pellet form, can be given to coincide with the four months of optimum growth – September to December in the Southern Hemisphere and April to October under glass and June to September in the Norther Hemisphere – after which little is required until repotting time and any deficiency can be corrected by liquid feeding.
- Fertigation or 'liquid feeding' is the administering of fertiliser in any regular application of irrigation water and – as it is very controllable – it is the method most frequently used in large scale horticultural projects. For small growers the immersion method of watering previously recommended is suitable for this type of administration.
- Foliar feeding is only recommended where ventilation and air movement are good. As with any application of liquid to the leaves, it should be administered in the early morning, on a dull day or at such a time as it is able to dry before evening, thus lessening the possibility of botrytis or other fungal infection.

Containers

Pelargoniums are grown in a wide variety of containers – in window-boxes, hanging baskets, pots and novelty containers of many kinds and materials. All of these are practicable as long as they have adequate drainage.

- Clay pots have a pleasant natural appearance, they are heavy and provide a solid, untippable base. They are, however, easily broken or chipped, hard to clean and, due to their porosity, the contents dry out quickly.
- Plastic pots are the most widely used, as they are cheap, light, clean and easy to stack in a small storage area. They do not dry out as rapidly as clay pots and therefore need less watering. Plastic pots come in many colours, but dark neutral shades are the best complement to brightly coloured pelargoniums. For the sake of stability, the squatter wider-based types are preferable.
- Concrete troughs, tubs and urns are obtainable for permanent positions in the garden. They can look very decorative and elegant and are certainly very enduring.
- Timber is much used for larger containers such as planter-boxes, window-boxes and half-barrels. It can be used to construct any shape required, it can be scrubbed and disinfected easily and is lighter to move than concrete. Timber containers have to be treated with a preservative to prevent rotting – creosote should not be used for this purpose as it is poisonous to pelargoniums. It is important to ensure that any constructed container has plenty of drainage holes in the base.
- Wire hanging baskets are still used, though plastic ones have recently gained wider favour. Wire containers have to be lined with spagnum moss or black plastic (with drainage holes) to contain the mix. They dry out rapidly and need to be watered almost every day.

In fact plant containers can, with a little ingenuity, be made from practically anything – hollowed out logs, old kettles or old wheelbarrows all make attractive containers. Glazed ceramic pots, though expensive, are particularly suitable as they combine the pleasant appearance and weight of clay pots with the non-porous attributes of plastic.

Positions and Uses in Gardens

The Geranium family can be used for decorative purposes almost anywhere in the garden – some make effective bedding plants and can be used for borders and for ground cover; others can be grown in rockeries or on banks; they can be trailed down walls or trained as climbing plants; they can be grown in containers.

Container Gardens

Container gardens are becoming increasingly popular in this era of apartments, flats and units with little or no garden. Whether the environment is warm or cold, a place –

verandah, window-sill, sunroom patio, terrace or sun-deck – can usually be found for a container garden. Backyards and conservatories too, are places for pots and containers. Urns can be used in larger gardens and parks. Pelargoniums are ideal plants for container growing – evergreen and copiously flowering – they can be decorative all year round when grown in conservatories and greenhouses, by themselves or mixed with other plants. It is important to remember however, that they should be given shelter from strong winds and driving rain, that they should receive sunlight for about three-quarters of the day, and an adequate water supply is essential. Pots may be positioned on the ground or, as some variation in height can produce a more attractive display, on shelving, steps or wall brackets.

If planting pelargoniums in containers with other plants, they will need to be plants which like a similar type of soil – it is no use trying to grow pelargoniums around camellias, rhododendrons or azaleas which thrive on acid soils.

Beds

Beds of zonal pelargoniums are colourful through spring and summer, they are also tough and tolerant of many conditions, though not at their best in a wet season when heavy rain and humidity can make the flowers rot. If the dead flowers are promptly removed many more will soon form.

When planning a bed the following points should be borne in mind:
- Note should be taken of the soil type and it should be adapted if necessary (see page 11).
- Flowers of one colour are more effective than mixed colours.
- Plant out as soon as frosts are over and the ground starts to warm up. Planting out too soon will retard growth or the plants may even be killed by frost. If the plants have been raised in a greenhouse allow them to harden-off before planting.
- Spraying regularly with a caterpillar repellent, such as carbaryl or permethrin, as soon as the first butterflies make an appearance, is recommended. A regular inspection of the under surface of leaves for any signs of rust is also advisable.
- If watering is necessary, flooding the ground is better than overhead sprinkling.
- After flowering is finished in the autumn, cuttings may be taken to grow new plants for the following year. In warm areas the original plants can continue to provide good displays for about three years if pruned and left in place. In colder areas, in some countries, it is an accepted practice to bury potted plants in the ground for the flowering period, then return them to the greenhouse for the cooler months.
- There are several cultivars, such as 'Paul Crampel' and 'Gustav Emich' (originally known as the Buckingham Palace Geranium because of the eye-catching scarlet-red beds of these plants which once stood in front of the palace), which have traditionally been used for bedding plants. Recently these have been changed to the new F1 hybrid seedlings 'Grenadier' and 'Adrette' and these, with other recently developed seedling plants 'Sprinter', 'Red Elite' and 'Scarlet Diamond' are gradually superseding cutting-grown cultivars as bedding plants. They are grown commercially and sold in packs for this purpose.
- Regal pelargoniums, due to their shorter flowering period and poor weather resistance, are less suitable as bedding plants.
- Variegated-leaved zonal pelargoniums can be used to good effect as bedding plants. They produce a multicoloured, patterned carpet, even when not in flower. In milder areas these can be ornamental throughout the winter months.

Borders

'Madame Salleron', a variegated, compact, low-growing, non-flowering cultivar, is often used as a border edging, sometimes without it being realised that it is a pelargonium. Many others are suitable, so long as they are of compact habit and are reasonably hardy in the district in which they are grown. Some miniatures, particularly the coloured-leaf varieties such as 'Golden Harry Hieover', make a decorative border in warmer areas or for the summer in cooler climates. The old Victorian habit of planting scented pelargoniums beside the path, to provide scent when brushed against, may be worth a revival.

Pelargoniums are sometimes placed singly in herbaceous borders, but not always with success, as the rich, well-manured soil for that type of border can lead to the plant producing abundant leaves and few flowers.

Banks, Ground Cover and Walls

Ivy-leaved pelargoniums are the obvious choice for these areas – they are natural sprawlers and can cover a large area in a short time. However, it should be remembered that the internodal length varies from cultivar to cultivar. The new seed-raised 'Summer Showers' has especially long internodes and its display is therefore rather diffuse. Banks that are hard to mow, rocky or rough areas that need a dense cover, bare walls that need decoration, stumps that need covering, are all situations for which the ivy-leaved pelargoniums are extremely useful. They provide many flowers over a long period and a contrast of evergreen foliage next to a lawn, yet they require little care – an occasional trim around the edges is often all that they need.

Several of the scented pelargoniums, such as *P. tomentosum*, *P. quercifolium* and the frost tender *G. incanum* (not itself a scented geranium, although it does have scented leaves), plus a huge range of frost-hardy geranium species and cultivars, can also make excellent, fast-growing, ground cover. When planting, bear in mind that the most vigorous of these plants will cover a square metre of ground in a year if kept weed-free. Once established they will effectively smother most further weed growth.

The well known pink-flowering, ivy-leaved pelargonium seen growing in many such areas is called 'Madame Crousse', but there are many other flower colours among the cultivars that can be used, ranging from white to deepest purple and through many shades of pink and red.

Climbing

While ivy-leaved pelargoniums are horizontal rather than vertical growers – and have no tendrils for clinging – they can be trained as climbers in frost-free areas or in conservatories if given suitable support. Coarse netting serves this purpose as their long shoots grow through and around the netting, and their natural growth pattern supports them. Ivy-leaved pelargoniums are adventurous, determined climbers; they can be seen, in many places, thrusting up through low picket fences, hedges and bushes; climbing up netting, around posts and letterboxes, or spread-eagled against the walls of houses – sometimes reaching almost to the eaves.

Although there is customarily a tendency to prune zonal pelargoniums so as to achieve compact growth structures, they can, where they incline towards straggly growth, be effectively trained as low climbers, or, if desired, as standards.

Standards or Tree Geraniums

Zonal or regal pelargoniums, like roses or fuchsias, can be trained as standards; the stems of pelargoniums, however, are not as strong and always have to be supported with a stake. To establish a standard plant:

- Choose a plant that has been raised from a cutting, has a strong single stem and a healthy terminal bud. When it reaches the stage of being potted on into a 7.5cm (5in) pot, a heavy clay pot is recommended as the plant will become top-heavy. Insert the stake at this stage.
- Remove all lateral growth until the desired height is reached, then remove the terminal bud to promote side growth of the crown.
- As each side shoot of the crown reaches 10 cm (4 in) in length, pinch out the tip buds, repeat this on all developing side shoots and forming flower buds until the desired size is achieved.
- Continue to remove lower leaves if they develop.
- Fertilise weekly.
- Grow at warm temperatures – 16°C (62°F) night and 21°C (70°F) day.

Hanging Baskets

Ivy-leaved pelargoniums, with their long drooping stems and free flowering habit, are the obvious choice for hanging baskets. All cultivars can be used, but some seem to branch more evenly than others and present a better balanced plant – 'Abel Carriere' and 'Sir A. Hort' are particularly recommended. Use can also be made of some of the smaller growing scented pelargoniums such as *P. fragrans* (nutmeg scented) and *P. odoratissimum* (apple scented) or geranium species such as *G. Incanum*, which make delightful and fragrant baskets.

Wire baskets or hanging plastic pots are customarily used for containers. If wire baskets are used they should be lined, either with black plastic (with holes for drainage) or dry sphagnum moss. Prior to planting, the basket should be filled with the required mix and left standing in water until thoroughly saturated. It is important never to let baskets dry out completely, as the moss shrinks and the filling mix can become dislodged. Always water by standing the basket in water – top-watered, the moss never gets completely saturated. Wire baskets need to be watered almost every day. While they may not be as aesthetically pleasing, plastic hanging pots are much easier to manage as they do not require such frequent watering, and the plastic is soon hidden by the trailing foliage.

Depending on the size of the basket, two, three or even four cuttings may be planted – in even a small basket a single cutting seems to provide a lop-sided effect.

As the plants grow, let the shoots grow level to the base of the basket, then pinch out the heads to encourage lateral growth of other shoots. Once a good supply of shoots has been achieved, let them grow to desired lengths.

In late autumn, cut the plants back to promote new growth the following year or take cuttings to overwinter in frost-free conditions for new baskets the following season. Top up the growing media – as this is inclined to shrink – and lightly mix in a sprinkling of lime.

With the appearance of new growth in the spring, start adding regular doses of liquid fertiliser to the water supply.

Window Boxes

Window boxes should be made of sturdy timber at least 20 mm (¾ in) thick. The timber can either be painted, stained or treated with timber preservative (except creosote). The box can be used either as a receptacle for potted plants, or filled with potting compost and used as a container for growing permanent plants. In the latter case, the box should be at least 30 cm (1 ft) deep and wide, it should have good drainage holes in the base – 1 cm (about ½ in) in diameter and spaced 15 to 20 cm (6 to 7¾ in) apart in two rows. It is important, for the purpose of watering, to ensure that the box is level.

Plants in window-boxes can be of almost any cultivar – trailing ivy-leaved, zonal pelargoniums or a mixture of both. Scented varieties are also pleasant though not so colourful.

Window boxes are usually thought of as being placed outside. An attractive alternative, however, is a box which can be positioned along the inside of a window, and which can be used for displaying miniatures. Made of plastic or ceramics, such boxes can occasionally be purchased, alternatively they can be home-made of any waterproof material or, at least, lined with such.

Rockeries

Erodiums, geraniums and pelargoniums all have a place in the rockery; erodiums and low-growing geranium cultivars are particularly suitable.

While most zonal pelargoniums are unsuitable for rockery planting due to their height, miniatures planted in a group can form a colourful patch.

Ivy-leaved pelargoniums are often used but many cultivars can, unless frequently trimmed, quickly overgrow other plants. There are several miniature forms, such as 'Gay Baby' and 'Sugar Baby', or some with a more restricted growth pattern, 'Sunset Marble' or 'Crocodile' (both of which also have attractive variegated leaves) which are suitable.

The compact growing scented species *P. fragrans*, with its small grey-green leaves and many white flowers, is another that should be considered.

Winter Protection for Pelargoniums

In all but the most suitable climates (those approaching the environmental conditions of their native habitat, South Africa), pelargoniums need some form of protection during the winter, even if only a porch, sunroom or sunny window-sill. Pelargoniums growing outside, pruned back for the winter, may, with a plastic or glass cloche protection, survive in a cold district.

If the temperature in winter falls below 1°C, heated glasshouses are needed – the temperature should ideally be kept between 7°C and 15°C (45°C and 60°C). Ventilation should be good and humidity kept low.

In districts with mild winter climates, cold frames, or unheated glass or plastic houses, are all that are necessary. Alternatively, a structure with a plastic roof and windcloth walls is often quite enough to protect pelargonium plants from stormy winter weather and mild frosts, and is relatively inexpensive.

If plants are kept in a glasshouse during hot summer weather, some form of shading is necessary to prevent sunburn and wilting, and ventilators should be left open.

Within the glasshouse, benches are useful for easy care of plants. The best display of plants is achieved with tiered shelving (Figure 7). Where available, long-run, square-ridged, roofing iron is extremely useful for shelves, as the ends can be turned up to form waterproof tanks which simplify the watering process considerably (capillary water matting or a plastic tube irrigation system – see Figures 5 and 6 shown earlier), as long as adequate provision is made for draining off excess water. Care should be taken that they are perfectly level, and that all pots are within easy reach.

Figure 7 Tiered shelving and water troughs. Tiered shelving is a good method of display. If the shelves are made with long-run iron (sealed at both ends), these tanks can be filled with water for simple watering: provision should be made for the removal of surplus water

It is always preferable to see the plants that you are buying. Sometimes, however, they have to be bought sight unseen from catalogues and arrive by post.

If possible, when buying pelargoniums, select healthy, sturdy plants with balanced, well-branched foliage, as these suggest good root development. The occasional yellow or dried leaf is natural, but avoid any plants which have yellow margins around several leaves – this could be an indication of root rot. Any plants which have blackening of the stem (indicating black-leg), or spotted or contorted leaves (suggesting virus infection) should also be discarded.

If the plants have to be delivered by mail, order them during the cooler parts of the year – autumn or spring – as plants travelling in the summer can arrive in a poor condition. On arrival, mailed plants will be in a state of shock and should not be immediately planted outside but 'nursed' in a pot until they recover. Such plants are usually newly rooted cuttings and they will need a warm, sheltered place in a glasshouse, a sunroom, or on a window-sill, to develop a good root system. They should not be given liquid manure until they are established. Prior to being planted outside they should have grown sufficiently for at least one cutting to be taken – not only does this ensure that adequate growth has taken place, it also provides a back-up should the original plant fail to establish.

Plants offered for sale in shops are often in poor condition. Some shops do not stock pelargoniums at all as it is maintained that they do not keep. This apparent inability to maintain growth is generally because they are placed among the other plants and frequently top-watered with sprinklers. They would have a greater chance of survival if kept together in a group by themselves, or placed with the cacti and succulents in a sunny position – a soggy, shaded pelargonium is not a happy plant.

If the plant being purchased is purely for decorative purposes, and the purchaser is not a collector interested only in named cultivars, there are now becoming increasingly available many plants commercially grown from seed. These should be bought just as the first flowers are opening, it will then be possible to distinguish flower colour and form. Choose one that has plenty of branching stems and several flower heads

formed, with others forming, this will ensure a long flowering plant.

Propagation

Pelargoniums must be one of the easiest plants to propagate. There are several propagation methods – growing from seed, rooting from tip or stem cuttings, or multiplying by ground or air layering. The two major methods are propagation from cuttings and from seed. Grafting, though possible, gives no great advantage and is only very occasionally used when a novelty plant is required – for example several cultivars growing on a single plant.

Cuttings

New plants can easily be raised by taking cuttings from a parent plant. Cuttings will show the same characteristics as the cultivar from which they are taken, whereas home-saved seeds will not be true to type except if produced under rigidly controlled breeding situations.

Pelargonium cuttings, given suitable conditions, will put out roots at any time of the year. Autumn is, however, generally considered to be the most convenient season – after flowering is over and at a time when pruning and shaping are necessary. If the newly struck cuttings are kept inside during the winter months they will be ready to plant out in the spring as healthy well-started plants. If cuttings are taken during the summer they are more prone to fungal disease, and if taken during the winter they will take a considerably longer time to form roots. Cuttings may be taken in the spring for later flowering and for the propagation of variegated-leaved cultivars which may have been used during the winter for decorative purposes, it thus gives them ample time to develop into well grown, leafy plants before the following winter.

Cuttings can vary in length, but 100 mm (4 in) is about average. Choice of size varies with the growth pattern of the plant – cuttings from miniature plants may be as small as 35 mm (1½ in) as these plants are miniature by virtue of their shortened internodes. Whatever the length, however, the cutting should have three or four nodes and come from healthy, disease-free stock.

Cuttings can be taken either from the tip of a growing branch or from the stem. Tip cuttings generally develop more quickly and form a more evenly balanced plant than stem cuttings. The latter method is often more convenient when taking cuttings from the ivy-leaved pelargoniums, as the structure of their long branches, cut off at pruning time, lends itself to this type of division.

All cuttings should be taken with a sharp clean instrument. A satisfactory method is to use a single-sided razor blade which has been kept immersed in methylated spirits in a lidded plastic container. The razor blade should be changed between each plant, the previously used blade being dropped back into the sterilizing container. This method reduces any spread of infection and helps to sterilize the wound on the parent plant where the cutting has been detached. Procedures for taking cuttings are shown in Figure 8:

- Cuttings should be made just below a node.
- All lower leaves and stipules should be removed, leaving only three or four top leaves (including young shooting leaves).
- Remove all flowers or developing flower shoots.
- The end of the cutting that is to be planted can be lightly dusted with zineb or benomyl to prevent fungal disease and a rooting hormone powder (softwood) to promote root development, although neither of these two stages are absolutely necessary and their efficaciousness is sometimes doubtful.
- Place each cutting into the damp rooting mix – this can be just coarse sand, a half sand and half peat mix, or a commercial potting mix.
- It is advisable to use a separate small pot for each cutting to lessen the chance of root damage when they are potted on.
- Each cutting should be pushed down into the loose, damp mix which is then pressed down firmly around the cutting.
- Label each cutting individually.

Figure 8 Taking cuttings from pelargoniums

Take tip cuttings of 10-15 cm (4-6 in), or 3-4 nodes in length. Cut just below a node

Remove all stipules, lower stalks and leaves, except the top 3 or 4

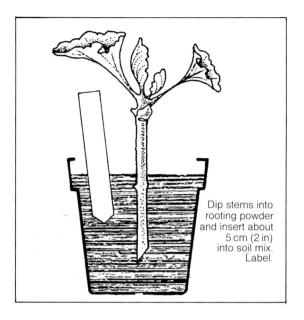

Dip stems into rooting powder and insert about 5 cm (2 in) into soil mix. Label.

Cuttings root very quickly, often within a week, but it is preferable to leave them in their first pots for three weeks, by which time they will be well-rooted plants, ready to be transplanted.

If the cuttings have been placed in damp mix they should not need watering during the following week. All cutting containers should be kept in a plastic seed tray then, when watering is required, the whole tray can be immersed in a shallow tank of water and left until all the mix has been saturated, the tray should then be removed and allowed to drain. Do not allow the soil mix to dry out completely, but do not overwater.

It is important to remember that ventilation should be adequate at all times, in order to prevent a build-up of humidity which could encourage fungal diseases. Newly struck cuttings should be watched for the onset of black-leg or botrytis (see page 24).

Base-heated propagation units are not recommended, especially for regal pelargoniums.

Propagation from Seed

Until very recently all pelargoniums, except the seedlings grown in an effort to find new cultivars, were raised from cuttings. See-dlings did not grow true-to-type, and cutting-raised plants were quicker to flower than seedlings. In 1965, however, Pennsylvania State University Horticultural Department raised the first continuously true-to-type hybrid seed called 'Nittany Lion'. Since then many new cultivars have been developed and are continuing to be developed. 'Sprinter', one of the earliest, is readily available for sale in seed shops under the name of 'Pot Geranium'. Until the mid seventies the colour of 'Sprinter' was limited to red and salmon, but during the past few years many new colours have been produced. Other varieties such as 'Red Elite' and 'Cherie' are gradually appearing on the retail market and will, no doubt, soon supersede the older varieties. Seed-grown plants will now flower within fifteen weeks of planting, and continue to flower longer into the autumn than cutting-raised plants.

Seeds can be planted either in the autumn for spring planting, or in the spring for later flowering. When planting seeds:
- Sow the seeds 1 cm (⅜ in) deep in seed boxes, punnets or directly into individual tubs or pots. The germinating mix can be either a sterile 1-1-1, peat, perlite, soil mix or a commercially prepared seed raising mix.
- Germination may take place from 1 to 3 weeks after planting. The optimum conditions for germination are to keep the soil temperature at 22°C (74°F) and uniformly moist.
- If transplanting is necessary it should be undertaken at the first true leaf stage.
- While not essential, light gives quicker germination and stronger seedlings – it can be supplied by hanging a coolwhite fluorescent light 35 cm (15 in) above the seed bed, it should be turned on 16 to 24 hours per day, for the first 21 to 30 days from planting.
- While surface misting is permissible, bottom soaking is preferable. It is important that the planting medium is *never* allowed to dry out completely.
- After germination is complete, soil temperature should be reduced slowly to 15°C (60°F).
- Unchecked growth produces the best plants. This can be obtained by administering a regular liquid feeding programme in conjunction with the water supply, starting about 2 to 3 weeks after

germination. A balanced N.P.K. fertiliser of 20-20-20 is recommended. When flower buds start to appear, a raising of the potash supply and a lowering of the nitrogen is advantageous to diminish the leaf growth and increase the formation of flowers. This can be given in the form of potassium nitrate at a rate of 150 g per litre (24 oz per gallon) diluted at 1 in 200 and used instead of the N.P.K. solution.

Propagation of Geraniums and Erodiums

Propagation of geraniums and erodiums is basically the same as for pelargoniums. They can be grown from cuttings, division, or from seed, the only difference is in the appearance of the cutting (Figure 9). Unlike pelargoniums, the branches of geraniums and erodiums are at ground level and often form a clump rather than a branching plant. To obtain a cutting it is necessary to tear off a small clump with a heel from the main trunk, rather than taking it from the tip or stem of the plant. Remove any outer, dried or aged

leaves – to all intents and purposes, peeling the base of the cutting – dip it in rooting hormone powder, as with pelargonium cuttings, and insert the heel in the soil mix, pressing the soil firmly around the plant. The heel will root quite readily. Some seeds germinate quite quickly while others may take weeks, even months, to germinate.

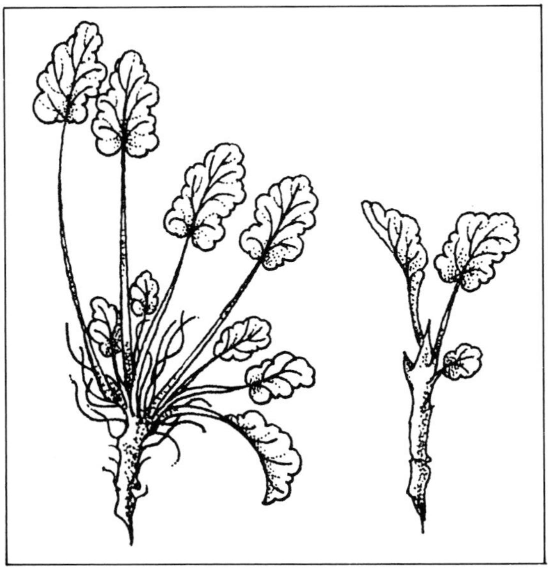

Layering

Though not a usual practice, a simple method for home gardeners – particularly if they do not have any facilities for propagation – is to form new plants by layering. Most pelargonium and some geranium plants can develop long branches, potentially each node on these branches can develop into a new plant. The procedure to follow for layering is shown in Figure 10.

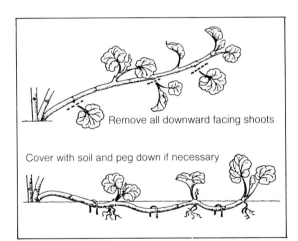

Figure 10

- Choose a stem which has fairly widely-spaced nodes.
- Lay it along the ground, still attached to the parent plant, in a shallow trench.
- Remove any downward facing shoots. Cut a small piece of the outer stem from the bottom side of each node and lightly dust the wound with rooting powder.
- Fill the trench with soil, covering the stem but letting any shoots remain above ground. Wire hoop staples can be placed between nodes to hold the branch in place if it tends to rise above the trench.

Figure 9
Cutting of Erodium reichardii *taken from a clump-growing plant.*
When the small shoots and mat of dying stems and elongated stipules are removed it will be seen that they are very similar to other Geraniaceae cuttings

- Roots should form readily at each wounded node and, when the top shoots have grown well, the branch can be cut between nodes to form several new plants.

General Care of Plants

Chapter 2 discussed the growing conditions required, but care of plants requires more than just putting them in the right environment, it requires day-to-day care – for example removing dead flower heads and yellow leaves, and the eradication and prevention of damage caused by pests and diseases. Probably the busiest time of the year is in the autumn – after the main flowering has finished but before the frosts come. This is the time for pruning, repotting and taking cuttings, for division and replanting and for trimming sprawling or invasive plants.

Repotting

Plants in pots, provided that they are given room to expand their root system, can last for several years. Second-year plants are generally the best and, although plants will last longer, re-taking cuttings so that second-year plants are available for display purposes, is good practice. A plant which needs repotting will have filled the pot with a mass of fibrous roots which extend beyond the drainage holes; the nutrients in the remaining soil are not sufficient for the needs of the larger plant, and growth ceases.

A simple rule is that a plant needs repotting, into a pot 3 cm (1 in) larger, once a year. This may need to be carried out twice in the first year as growth is quicker. When repotting:
- Put about 3 cm (1 in) of mix in the bottom of the new pot.
- Soak the plant well before repotting as moisture helps the mix to cling together and, when the pot is inverted, the rootball will be more inclined to come out in one piece. Care should be taken not to tease it apart – the less disturbance to the roots the better.
- Place the whole rootball on the soil in the new pot, check that the final soil level will be about 2 cm (¾ in) below the rim so as to ensure satisfactory watering. If the soil surface is too low, put more mix underneath; if the fibrous roots are visible above the soil around the stem, or if the plant is starting to lean sideways, plant it deeper into the new pot and put more mix on top. Unlike some plants, pelargoniums do not suffer from having their previous soil level covered and will often put out new roots from the newly-buried stem.
- Fill in the space around the rootball with new mix and tamp it down firmly.
- Prune the newly potted plant.

Pruning

The aim of any pelargonium grower is to produce a well-branched, sturdy, round-shaped plant, with a good supply of flowers. The main pruning is carried out in the autumn, though tip pruning in late winter and spring should be undertaken to promote side branching and bushy growth. The simple rules of pruning – which apply to most plants – are:
- Remove any dead or diseased branches, cutting right back to the parent branch.
- Clean out the centre of the plant, removing inward growing or crossing stems.
- Prune each stem to an outward facing bud.
- Use a clean sharp instrument – ensure that it is frequently sterilized.
- Always cut just above a node as new growth will spring from the node and any internodal tissue left above that new growth will die back, enhancing the possibility of disease entry.
- New shoots will appear, both at the top and from other nodes further down the stem; allow these shoots to grow until they are three or four nodes long, then pinch out the tips to encourage further branching.

Different species have their own idiosyncrasies and require slightly different treatment:
- Zonal pelargoniums, particularly garden plants, can be cut back very hard, leaving the stumps of several branches, each about four nodes long, see Figure 11. If they are vigorous they will have a good root system and will soon put out many new shoots. More delicate plants or those

in pots should be pruned less severely, and some leaves and shoots should be allowed to remain.

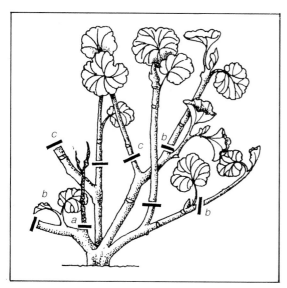

Figure 11 Pruning a zonal pelargonium
(a) cut out dead wood
(b) leave any low shoots
(c) cut back to each 3rd or 4th node

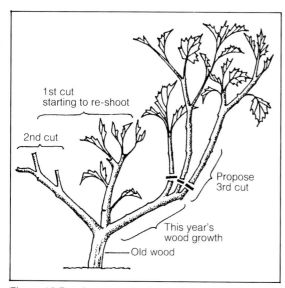

1st cut
starting to re-shoot

2nd cut

Propose 3rd cut

This year's wood growth

Old wood

Figure 12 Pruning a regal pelargonium

- Miniature and dwarf zonal pelargoniums grow at a much slower rate and consequently need little pruning. However, the centre of these plants can become overcrowded with branches and harbour disease – if this occurs the centre should be thinned out. Occasional light, tip pinching will encourage growth and branching.
- Regal pelargoniums can suffer from shock – and even die – if they are pruned too hard, especially if they are old, woody plants. It is preferable to half, or even third prune them at any one time, then allow the pruned portions to start shooting before completing the operation, see Figure 12.
- Among the scented cultivars and species of pelargoniums there are many different growth patterns. Where similar to the listed types, they should be pruned in the manner described. However, many do not require rigorous pruning, they only need an annual trim to produce the desired shape and tidy growth.

Pests, Diseases and Disorders

Pelargoniums are unfortunately prone to many diseases and disorders. While suitable sprays play an important part in counteracting the effects of these, they can arise from incorrect growing conditions and insufficient attention to plant hygiene. A well-grown, vigorous plant is always less susceptible to disease – good cultural practices are an important first line of defence. Greenhouse and growing areas should be kept clean and all waste matter – dead flowers, leaves, etc. – should be removed and burned. If spraying is necessary, it should be carried out when light levels are low – early in the morning or on dull days – and preferably not in the evening as moisture sitting on the leaves all night could be an encouragement to botrytis. It is just as important to spray under the leaves as on top.

Insects

Caterpillars
Several kinds of caterpillars are readily attracted to pelargoniums, particularly zonal pelargoniums. In a few days they can strip

a plant of all its greenery, chew the stems, eat young shoots and burrow through the flower buds – nothing escapes them.

As soon as the first cabbage butterflies are observed in late spring, start taking immediate preventative measures. A light dusting of derris dust can be useful as a deterrent, but it tends to spoil the appearance of the plant. There are many suitable insecticides on the market and, as brand names, formulations and restrictions change from time to time, advice should be sought as to those which are, currently, most suitable.

Greenfly (Many types)
Greenfly appear to prefer regal and some scented pelargoniums. They can be found in clusters around the young tips and cause distortion of leaves and buds by sucking the sap from the stem. They also carry virus diseases from plant to plant so it is imperative to eradicate them. Treat with pyrethrum, malathion or in the UK, the purpose-made aphicide pirimicarb which does not kill beneficial insects.

Mealy bugs (*Pseudococcus* species)
This sap-sucking insect has a preference for the ivy-leaved and zonal pelargoniums. The bugs congregate in the axils of leaves and are easily seen as small, white insects covered with a white, woolly secretion. Mild infections can be removed with a cotton wool bud soaked in methylated spirits – more widespread infections can be controlled with malathion.

Whitefly (*Trialeurodes vaporariorum*)
A frequent pest of plants under glass, whitefly can often be found on regal pelargoniums and on some scented species and cultivars. They are easy to distinguish as any disturbance of the leaves causes them to rise up in a cloud of tiny white insects, they also leave a sooty, black mould on the leaves. Pyrethrum, malathion and derris are effective, though several applications will be needed to eradicate further hatching insects.

Mice

Before leaving the world of predators, mention should be made of mice – unlikely though it may seem, they have been known to develop a liking for pelargonium stems and young seedlings. This hazard can be countered by using any of the customary methods of mouse control. Cats are not recommended as they may, in their turn, damage plants.

Fungi

Black stem rot or black-leg (*Pythium* species)
As the name suggests, black stem rot or black-leg is a black rotting of the stem – generally starting from below ground level and working its way upwards – especially in cuttings. Stem rot can also spread from an infected wound above ground level. It cannot be cured and the only effective treatment is to remove the area of infected tissue and to burn it. Infected cuttings – with any soil mix they were in – should be discarded. Plants with stem rot can, however, be saved by completely removing the blackened part and checking to make sure that there are no black or brown markings left in the centre of the stem – if further marking is evident cut further up the stem.

Optimum conditions for the growth of black stem rot are warmth, humidity, infected soil, and excessive soil moisture. Preventative measures include good ventilation, dipping the cuttings in fungicide, use of sterilized soil, and not overwatering.

Infected plants growing in the garden should be pulled out and burned, and the soil drenched with 10 per cent formalin solution.

Grey mould (*Botrytis cinerea*)
During periods of cool, humid weather, botrytis appears as a grey furry mould on flowers and leaves. It generally attacks the central florets of the blossoms first, causing browning, collapse and matting of the petals. Infected petals produce patches of yellow or brown when they fall onto the leaves below. Infected growth should be removed and burned to prevent the spread of spores – the plants should then be sprayed with benlate or a similar fungicide. Increased warmth, ventilation and spacing between plants will help to obviate its occurrence.

Leaf spot (*Cercospora brunkii*)
Leaf spots caused by cercospora are about 1/3 mm in diameter, sunken and pale green,

and turn grey with age. Control is obtained with benlate.

Rust (*Puccinia pelargonii-zonalis*)
This disease is very common in zonal pelargoniums, appearing as red-brown raised spots on the undersides of leaves. The spores are quickly spread by wind and water, especially in humid, warm weather. As its name suggests, rust is a disease of zonal pelargoniums only.

To guard against the spread of infection, damaged foliage should be placed in a suitable container – a paper or plastic bag – prior to removal for subsequent destruction. The whole plant or plants should then be sprayed with zineb or maneb (propiconazole in the UK) – both on the upper and under surfaces of the leaves, and on the soil surface.

Verticillium wilt (*Verticillium albo-atrum*)
This wilt is not very common, but can be contracted from infected soil. It causes the whole plant to wilt and will very quickly kill it. Destroy the plant – do not take cuttings as they will also be infected. Drench the soil with formalin.

Bacteria

Leafy gall (*Bacterium fascians*)
Leafy gall forms a cauliflower-like growth on the stem at ground level. The infliction does not appear to affect the growth of the plant nor does it seem to spread very rapidly. However, it is unsightly and does infect several other garden flower species, therefore it is probably advisable to destroy any infected plants as there does not seem to be any cure. Cuttings can be taken from the plant without any sign of the disease being carried on.

Bacterial leaf spot (*Pseudomonas cichorii*)
The slightly raised spots of bacterial leaf spot have tan centres and a yellow halo, they spread when the leaves are wet and cease to spread when the leaves are dry. If leaf spot is observed, infected areas should be pruned off or – if badly infected – the plant destroyed. Regular copper sprays prevent this bacterium from gaining a foothold.

Viruses

Several different viruses can infect pelargoniums and, while they do not kill the plant, they cause distortion, crinkling and spotting of the leaves. Viral infections are spread by aphids, or by infected pruning or cutting instruments. Care should be taken when buying plants to ensure that they are not virus infected. Cuttings should not be taken from infected plants and, if the plants are not of a rare, highly prized variety, it is advisable to destroy them. It is, however, almost impossible to avoid the universal presence of the soil-borne pelargonium leaf-curl virus in older varieties; this only causes some minimal puckering of the leaves, but at the same time, reduces vigour and flowering capacity, and promotes a lower strike rate from cuttings.

Some viruses, paradoxically, can produce very decorative effects by causing a light veining of the leaves – as can be seen in such cultivars as 'Crocodile', 'White Mesh' or 'Wantirna'.

Nutritional Deficiencies

Nutritional deficiencies can appear in older plants which have not been adequately fertilised. The cure is to dress the plant or plants with either a general fertiliser or with the mineral that appears to be deficient. Typical deficiencies are:
- Nitrogen – leaf size is smaller and they are of a light, yellow-green colour.
- Phosphorus – the leaves go dark green, almost a red-purple colour (reddening of the leaves can also be caused by a sudden drop in temperature).
- Potassium – the leaves become grey-green, with mottled, dead spots and margins.
- Magnesium – old leaves become yellowish between green veins.
- Iron – young leaves become yellowish between green veins.

This chapter can only introduce a very small number of plants from this vast family and from its many cultivars. The ones listed are chosen from those which are readily obtainable and which probably will be of greatest interest to the home gardener. The only exception to this rule is the section on sarcocaulons and monsonias which is included for the benefit of those interested in the whole Geraniaceae family. They are only rarely obtainable from specialist nurseries.

The common feature of the family Geraniaceae is the elongated fruit or schizocarp, which has five single locules (mericarps) each with one seed. The family is divided into five genera:

- *Sarcocaulon*, in which the flower is actinomorphic and has fifteen fertile stamens. They have permanent, spiny petioles and woody stems.

- *Monsonia*, in which the flowers are actinomorphic with fifteen fertile stamens.

- *Erodium*, in which the flowers are circular (actinomorphic) with ten stamens, only five of which are fertile.

- *Geranium*, in which the flower is actinomorphic with ten stamens all of which are fertile.

- *Pelargonium*, in which the flower is symmetrical in only one plane (zygomorphic) with a nectar spur, it has ten stamens of which not more than seven are fertile.

The genus *Pelargonium* is subdivided into sixteen sub-genera, of which three are of particular interest to the gardener:
- Ciconium, from which the zonal pelargoniums derive.
- Dibrachya, from which the ivy-leaved pelargoniums derive.
- Pelargonium, from which the regal pelargoniums derive.

In the pages that follow, the zonal and ivy-leaved pelargonium cultivars have been classified according to types, but the regal pelargoniums, which are all very similar, have been divided into groups according to colour.

Sarcocaulons and monsonias
Erodiums
Geraniums
Zonal pelargoniums, general
Zonal pelargoniums, single
Zonal pelargoniums, semi-double, including Irenes and Fiats
Zonal pelargoniums, double
Zonal pelargoniums, Stellar
Zonal pelargoniums, Cactus and Rosebud
Zonal pelargoniums, Deacons (floribundas) and Highfields
Zonal pelargoniums, miniatures
Zonal pelargoniums, vari-petalled and Bird's-egg
Zonal pelargoniums, variegated leaved
Ivy-leaved pelargoniums, general
Ivy-leaved pelargoniums, single and semi-double
Ivy-leaved pelargoniums, double
Ivy-leaved pelargoniums, variegated and miniature
Hybrid ivy-leaved pelargoniums
Regal pelargoniums, general
Regal pelargoniums, Pinks and Whites
Regal pelargoniums, Reds and Oranges
Regal pelargoniums, Mauves and Purples
Pelargonium species
Scented pelargoniums
Seed-grown hybrid pelargoniums
Oddments

Sarcocaulons (Bushman's candle, candle bush, Bushman's thorn)

The name sarcocaulon derives from the Greek, *Sarco* fleshy, and *Caulon* stem or stalk, and refers to the thick fleshy stalk of this plant. The popular names arise from the fact that they were used as firewood and a form of lighting by the native South African Bushmen, and it is interesting to note that modern investigation has revealed that the resin contained in the waxy covering of the branches is composed of 18 per cent pure petroleum and 54 per cent pure alcohol, with traces of volatile oil and magnesium.

There are twelve species, of which the following are the best known:
S. burmanii, S. ciliatum, S. inerme, S. patersonii, S. rigidum, S. spinosum, S. vanderietiae.

Sarcocaulon species are found in Namibia and the Eastern Cape area of South Africa, generally growing in thin soil, or sand, over a gravelly sub-stratum in dry, rocky areas.

Sarcocaulons are classified as sub-shrubs and their average height is between 12 and 24 cm (5 and 10 in). They have a fleshy stem and horizontal, rigid branches, a waxy epidermis and permanent spiny petioles and woody stems. The flowers are single, solitary and stalked and vary in colour between white, pink, red or yellow, according to species. The plants are almost leafless for the greater part of the year but, during the wet season, bear small, kidney-shaped leaves, simple entire and stalked.

New plants can be propagated easily from cuttings or from seed, but are very slow growing. They should be watered only during the autumn and early winter and kept dry for the remaining months of the year.

S. patersonii

Monsonia

Monsonia, named after Lady Anne Monson, a keen botanist and correspondent of Linnaeus, who named the plant. There are forty species of this small plant with a soft stem widely distributed throughout the African continent and India, thirty of which are to be found in South Africa. It appears to be little used in cultivated situations.

S. inerme

S. cilatum

Erodiums

The name erodium derives from the Greek *Erodios* meaning heron which refers to the sixty species of erodiums found growing mainly in Mediterranean countries, though they are also represented in the flora of America, Africa, Australia and New Zealand.

Those grown in garden situations are generally low-growing, clumpy plants suitable for ground cover or for use in rock gardens. They like sunny, well-drained positions and prefer dry, sandy soils.

Plants can be propagated by cuttings, or by division in autumn, or from seeds planted in the spring.

Colours can vary from white through several shades of pink and mauve, though there are some species with yellow and blue flowers.

Species used in gardens are:

E. chamaedryoides (also known as *E. reichardii*) *roseum*, height 15 cm (6 in), forms small tidy clumps about 30 cm (12 in) across with many small pink flowers.

E. chrysanthum, has fern-like, silver-grey foliage and yellow flowers.

E. corsicum, height 10 cm (4 in), grey-green foliage and small pink flowers.

E. hymenodes, height 15 to 20 cm (6 to 9 in), white to pale pink flowers with green, hairy foliage.

E. macredenum, height 15 cm (6 in), violet flowers.

E. manescavii, height 15 to 20 cm (6 to 9 in), purple-red flowers with green, fern-like leaves.

E. pelargoniflorum, height 30 cm (12 in), white flowers.

E. hymenodes

E. chamaedryoides

Geraniums (crane's bill)

The geranium is named from the Greek *Geranos* for crane. As suggested by its common name the seed pod resembles a crane's bill.

There are between three and four hundred species, both annuals and perennials, of the genus *Geranium* growing in temperate areas throughout the world. The perennials tend to grow in cool-temperate areas and the annuals in the warmer-temperate areas.

The majority of species range from 30 to 120 cm (12 to 46 in) and grow in grasslands and woodland margins. They generally grow in clumps though some have a spreading habit.

Leaves are on long stalks, round in shape and palmately lobed.

Flowers are round shaped and five-petalled, varying in colour from white to purple – or occasionally red – and in many shades of pink and mauve.

Geraniums grow in any well-drained soil and prefer a sunny to slightly shaded situation. Plants can be propagated by cuttings, division or from seeds planted in spring.

G. anemonifolium – this name embraces both *G. maderense* and *G. palmatum*, the former name indicative of their original habitat in the island of Madeira. They are short-lived perennials usually dying after flowering, they are easily grown from seed and will sometimes flower in their first year, but more often in their second year. They are slightly frost tender but can withstand droughts.

Height 1 m (39 in), leaves resemble those of an anemone, though much larger, reaching 30 to 60 cm (12 to 25 in) across, *G. maderense* being larger than *G. palmatum*. The flowers are borne on a tall, central panicle which carries several hundred flowers, each 4 to 5 cm (1½ to 2 in) across; flower colour, mauve-pink with purple centre.

G. endressii – from the Pyrenees.
Height 30 to 50 cm (12 to 20 in); leaves deeply lobed and toothed; flowers, pink and 3 cm (1¼ in) across. Several hybrid forms, the best known being *G. x oxonianum* 'Claridge Druce' which is slightly larger and more robust than its parents. *G. versicolor* x *G. endressii*.

G. macrorrhizum – from southern Europe.
Height 20 to 40 cm (8 to 16 in); tuberous rooted; purple-red flowers 2 to 3 cm (about 1 in) wide; lobed leaves which turn reddish in the autumn. Originally grew among rocks in shady mountainous areas. Fairly drought resistant.

An extract from this plant was used, in times past, for tanning leather.

G. renardii – from the Caucasus.
Height 20 to 30 cm (8 to 12 in); forms mounds of sage-green, felted leaves; flowers white-veined with purple, 4 cm (1½ in) across. Found on rock cliffs, prefers to live among rocks in meagre soils and cool climates.

G. dalmaticum – from Yugoslavia and Albania.
Height 12 cm (5 in); flowers, fragrant, pink, 2.5 cm (1 in) across; leaves 3 cm (1¼ in), forms in mats with flowers held above on long stems. Suitable for rockeries.

G. sylvaticum – from Europe and N. Turkey.
Height up to 60 cm (24 in); forms in clumps with deeply lobed and toothed leaves; flowers, bluish-purple and 3 cm (1¼ in) across. Sun or light shade.

G. sanguineum – from Europe (generally from limestone country).
Low-growing, mat-like plant; red-purple flowers, 2 to 4 cm (1 to 2 in) wide; rhizomatous roots; leaves deeply lobed. The variety with smaller pink flowers *G. sanguineum* var. *striatum* (formerly known as *lancastrense*).

G. robertianum – the 'Herb Robert' of the English countryside, though also native to N. Africa, the Himalayas and China.
Small red-purple flowers; ferny foliage and unpleasant scent; spreads very rapidly and can be classified as a weed in the wrong position; attractive in an orchard or shrubbery where it cannot become too invasive.

G. pratense – from Europe, Siberia and China.
Tall perennial; height 75 to 120 cm (30 to 48 in), known as meadow crane's bill, finely cut leaves and flowers 3 to 4 cm (1¼ to 2 in) across, blue to white; prefers limey or chalky ground and sun or light shade.

G. incanum – from South Africa.

Height 30 cm (12 in); leaves deeply cut and feathery; purple flowers 2 to 3 cm (1 to 1½ in) across carried in abundance through spring and summer; quick and attractive, frost-tender ground cover.

G. traversii – from coastal cliffs on the Chatham Islands.

Height 15 cm (6 in); forms clumps of light-green, silky leaves; pink or white flowers 2 to 3 cm (1 to 1½ in). The hybrid with *G. endressii* is called *G.* x *riversleaianum* 'Russell Prichard' and has the silky leaves of *G. traversii* and larger flowers of deeper pink. Slightly frost tender.

G. renardii

G. endressii

G. macrorrhizum

G. incanum

G. sylvaticum

G. traversiii

G. dalmaticum

G. sanguineum

Zonal Pelargoniums (zonal geraniums) *P. x hortorum* (Bailey)

Zonal pelargoniums are hybrids derived from several members of the pelargonium sub-genus Ciconium. Of these, *P. inquinans* is the principal parent plant. It is found in shallow, shaley soil on either side of the Fish River in South Africa. Other species, which have contributed to the development of zonal pelargoniums are *P. zonale, P. hybridum, P. frutetorum* and possibly *P. scandens*, all found in either the coastal scrub or on sparse hillsides of Cape Province.

The name 'zonal' applies, not as was first thought to the part descent from *P. zonale*, but to the dark rings or zones on the leaves. However, not all zonals have a ring – in some varieties it is absent, in others it is just a faint marking, while in yet others it is large and almost black.

The heights of these plants vary considerably between the different cultivars, but may be up to a metre (39 in). The stems are succulent and upright in growth, the older ones become slightly woody. The leaves are cordate and shallowly lobed, fleshy and slightly furry. Flowers are born in umbels, each inflorescence carried on a single stem arising from a node or leaf axil. The stem can carry over one hundred flowers, although commonly only about twenty are formed. Each flower can be either single, semi-double or double, and there are several variations in shape. Colours are in many shades, ranging from white, pink and red to mauve. The main flowering season is spring to early summer. Flowering takes place later in cooler climates and, under glass, flowers can be expected at any time of the year.

Zonal Pelargoniums – Single

A single flower has five petals, usually equal in size, but sometimes the two upper petals are smaller than the three lower ones. The colouring on the petals sometimes shows veining in a slightly deeper tone.

Single zonals should be planted where there is adequate shelter as the blossoms will shatter in a wind.

Cultivars
White
'Argyle'
'Edward Humphries'
'Marie Plummer'
'Queen of the Whites'

Pink
'Ascot' – salmon, large.
'Black Cox' – rose pink, dark leaves.
'Black Jubilee' – salmon, dark leaves.
'Candlewick' – apricot pink, large.
'Lady Folkestone' – fuchsene pink and white.
'Little Primula' – pale pink and white.
'Salmon Read' – salmon, dark band on leaf.
'Sir Philip Sydney' – pale pink.

Orange
'Jane Campbel' – pure orange, large.
'Soldiers Tunic' – bright orange.
'Skelly's Pride' – salmon-orange, serrated edging.
'Willingdon Gem' – orange-red with white eye.

Red
'Maloja' – poppy red.
'Maxim Kovalevski' – vermilion.
'Rev. Atkinson' – dark red.
'Antoine Crozy' – scarlet.
'Dublin rosy' – magenta.
'Feuriesse' – scarlet, very large.
'Victorious' – crimson.

Purple
'Prince of Wales' – Tyrian purple, upper petals based red.

'Queen of Whites'

'Little Primula'

Lady Folkestone'

'Feuriesse '

'Willingdon Gem'

'Marie Plummer'

Zonal Pelargoniums – Semi-Double

Semi-double flowers have more than five petals but not more than eight. They include the Irene and Fiat groups.

The Irenes were developed in America. They are very suitable for bedding plants and outside growing as they are strong growing with a low, spreading growth habit and produce many flowers. They are distinguished by their cup-shaped flower.

The Fiats were developed in France at the beginning of this century from a mutant plant. They have serrated petals which give them a carnation-like appearance. Fiats are delicate and should be regarded as a greenhouse pot plant. All the Fiat cultivars are different shades of pink.

Cultivars
White
'Apple Blossom' – shaded salmon on white.
'White Frills' – frilled edge.
'White Magic' – large flowers.

Pink
'Blossom Time' – pale coral.
'Lady Ilchester' – pale rose.
'Brocade' – deep pink, white centre.
'Obergaertner' – pale magenta, white centre.
'Bess' – salmon.
'California Pink Giant' – bright pink, white edge.
'Elizabeth Bode' – salmon, large.

Orange
'Orange Glow' – salmon-orange, compact.
'Orange Ricard' – orange-red, large.

Purple
'Le Lutin' – purple shot with red.
'Glorious' – tyrian purple.

Red
'Gustav Emich' – orange-scarlet.
'Mentmore' – red-salmon.
'Aztec' – vermilion, large.
'Holmes C. Miller' – deep red, large.

Irenes
'Apache' – dark red.
'Firebrand' – fire red.
'Jeweltone' – rich, deep red.
'Modesty' – pure white.
'Party Dress' – pale, rose pink.
'Showgirl' – bluish red.

Fiats
'Princess Fiat' – pale pink.
'Fiat' – coral pink.
'Fiat Royal' – palest pink.

'White Frills'

'Obergaertner'

'Party Dress'

'Modesty'

'Princess Fiat'

'Brocade'

Zonal Pelargoniums – Double

Double flowers have more than eight petals to each flower. The cultivars listed below are just a small selection from the many that are available.

Cultivars
White
'Wedding Day' – pure white.
'Gardenia' – satiny white.
'Joy' – white, flecked with salmon.
'Always' – cream, flecked pink.
'Gracious Lady' – white, flushed with lilac.
'Hermine' – green, tinge to white.

Pink
'Anne Richards' – creamy pink.
'American Double Dip' – pink and white.
'A. E. Bond' – apricot.
'Countess Maritza' – coral-salmon, large.
'Cameo' – white and pink.
'Exquisite' – bright coral.
'Derryl Sinclair' – frilly pink.
'Liberté' – pale pink.
'Treasure' – soft salmon.

Orange
'Profusion' – soft orange, petal reverse is paler.
'Gallant' – orange-salmon.
'Orange Parade' – orange.
'Gleam' – soft orange, large.
'Halloween' – soft orange, large, white centre.

Purple
'Festiva Maxima' – purple.
'Kardinal Raviselly' – deep mauve.
'Royal Purple' – purple.

Red
'Challenge' – deep red with white centre.
'Crimson Silk' – guardsman red.
'Fritz Anders' – crimson.
'Fireglow' – orange-scarlet, large.
'Garnet' – very dark red.
'Irish Hunt' – brick red.
'Melva Bird' – dark crimson.
'Missouri' – bright red.
'Pura Pura' – crimson.
'Zinc' – compact, bright red.

'Orange Parade'

'Karl Hegele'

'Festiva Maxima'

'Joy'

'Pura Pura'

'American Double Dip'

'Fritz Anders'

'Profusion'

Zonal Pelargoniums – Stellars (Staphs, star geraniums, five fingers or Both's hybrids)

The Stellars are a group of hybrids. The name refers to the shape of the leaf which has points like a star.

The flowers can be single or double, with the lower petals wedge shaped and the upper petals forked and narrow.

The Stardust group are Stellar varieties which can now be grown from F.1. hybrid seed.

Cultivars
White
'Arctic Star' – single, large head.
'Snowflake' – double.

Red
'Evening Star' – single, scarlet.
'Fairy Fire' – single, red and white.
'Grenadier' – double, scarlet.
'Red Demon' – single, red, small.
'Fandango' – double, crimson.

Purple
'Purple Star'

Pink
'Bird Dancer' – pale salmon, single, compact growth.
'Cathay' – single, salmon.
'Fairy Phlox' – single, phlox pink.
'Fairy Rose' – single, rose pink.
'Pink Star' – single, pale pink.
'Pixie Prince' – double, pink.
'Ade's Elf' – single, medium pink, large flower.
'Morning Star' – pale salmon, strong grower.
'Supernova' – double, lilac pink, large.
'Telstar' – double, salmon, narrow petals.

Orange
'Orange Pixie' – double, orange scarlet.
'Ragtime' – double, burnt orange.
'Golden Staph' – single, orange-red, gold zoned leaf.

Group of Stellars

'Red Stardust'

'Fairy Fire'

'White Star'

'Pink Star'

'Fandango'

Zonal Pelargoniums – Cactus and Rosebud

The Cactus and Rosebud pelargoniums are two groups of cultivars presenting unusual petal formations. Cactus pelargoniums, sometimes called pointsettia geraniums, have petals which are furled convexly giving the impression of quills. The Rosebud pelargoniums are a distinctively double form having approximately one hundred petals to each flower, they never open out completely and thus resemble rosebuds.

The origins of these mutations are unknown but Rosebud geraniums have been mentioned in geranium literature for over a hundred years, and Cactus since the turn of the century. Both groups are rather delicate so it is preferable to keep them for pot plant culture.

'Cactus' Cultivars
White
'Noel' – double.
'Silver Star' – single.

Pink
'Mrs Slater Bevis' – double, pink.
'More Mischief' – double, pale salmon.
'Morning Star' – apricot.

Orange
'Tangerine'

Red
'Red Cactus' – single, red.
'Spit fire' – red with variegated leaves.

Purple
'Star of Persia' – crimson-purple.

Rosebud Cultivars
'Apple Blossom Rosebud' – cream
   edged with pink.
'Rosebud Supreme' – salmon with white
   reverse.
'Scarlet Rosebud' – scarlet.
'Black Pearl' – dark red.
'Red Rambler' – red reversed with white.
'Plum Rosebud' – wine red.
'Cerise Rosebud' – cerise.

'Mrs Slater Bevis'

'Tangerine'

'Noel'

'Apple Blossum Rosebud'

'Cerise Rosebud'

'Scarlet Rosebud'

'Rosebud Supreme'

Zonal Pelargoniums – Deacons and Highfields

Both of these types have a compact, bushy habit of growth with round shaped plants and many branches. The Deacons are sometimes called floribundas as they produce many heads of flowers over a prolonged flowering period. They have semi-double flowers, smallish but abundant. The Highfields are sturdy, short plants with large flower heads.

Both types are strong growing plants that never look untidy, excellent for border or container growing.

Deacon Cultivars
White
'Arlon' – white.
'Picotee' – white with pink edging.

Pink
'Coral Reef' – coral pink.
'Minuet' – pale pink.
'Constancy' – light pink.
'Bonanza' – mauve-pink.
'Gala' – pale salmon.
'Romance' – neon rose.
'Trousseau' – salmon.
'Lilac Mist' – pale lilac-pink.

Orange
'Mandarin' – orange.
'Peacock' – orange-red with variegated leaf.

Red
'Fireball' – bright scarlet.
'Regalia' – ruby red.
'Summertime' – soft red.

Highfield Cultivars
'Attracta' – double, white shaded with salmon.
'Candy Floss' – double, pink.
'Contessa' – double, deep salmon.
'Festival' – double, rose pink.
'Flair' – double, bright scarlet.
'Pearl' – single, dark pink shaded with white.
'Promise' – single, pale pink with white eye.

'Fireball'

'Peacock'

'Mandarin'

'Bonanza'

'Picotee'

'Candy Floss'

'Lilac Mist'

Zonal Pelargoniums – Miniature and Dwarf

These pelargoniums rarely exceed 20 cm (8 in) in height; they are ideal as small colourful pot plants where space is limited; they are well suited to sunny window-sills and never grow too large for these positions.

Although it appears that miniatures were known as early as the late eighteenth century, it is only since the beginning of the twentieth century that they have been propagated commercially. Only since the second world war have they been extensively hybridised to produce the many and varied cultivars that are available today.

They come in a wide variety of colours, both in foliage and flowers, and are just as easy to propagate as the larger zonal types.

When they are small, 6 cm (2½ in) pots are suitable, but as they grow they will need repotting – 10 cm (4 in) pots are large enough when they reach maturity.

Cultivars
White
'Ambrose' – double, creamy white.
'Little Big Shot' – single, white, large flower. (Also available in red and salmon.)
'Snowbaby' – double, white.
'Rosebud Gem' – double rosebud form, white with touch of pink.

Pink
'Cranford Pink' – double, pink, dark leaves.
'Kleiner Liebling' – single, miniature flowers, deep pink.
'Salmon Black Vesuvius' – single, rose pink, dark leaves.
'Tu-tone' – double, pink and white.
'Baby Bird's-egg' – single, palest pink with deeper pink specks.
'Frills' – single, pink petals and dark leaves, both wavy.
'Jane Eyre' – double, pink, dark leaves.
'Jedda' – salmon pink, dark leaves.

Orange
'Cranford Fireboy' – double, orange-red.
'Festal' – double, orange-salmon, gold leaves.
'Hitcham' – double, bright orange.
'Orion' – double, orange-red, dark leaves.

Red
'Golden Harry Hieover' – single, scarlet, gold and bronze leaves.
'Cranford Bright Red' – single, red.
'Cranford Dazzle' – double, red.
'Blakesdorf' – single, red, thin petals and dark leaves.
'Cherie' – single, red and white.
'Picaninny' – single, red with white eye.
'Jaunty' – double, red with white eye.
'Playboy' – single, dark red.
'Silver Kewense' – single, crimson, white and green variegated leaves.

'Frills'

'Salmon Black Vesuvius'

44

'Blakesdorf'

'Cherie'

'Kleiner Liebling'

'Picaninny'

'Little Big Shot'

'Jaunty'

Zonal Pelargoniums – Vari-Petalled

Although this is not really a separate classification, quite a number of zonal pelargoniums have interesting multi-coloured flowers – striped, dotted, edged or reversed with a different colour. Many flowers tend to have a slightly different shading towards the centre, but in some instances this is so pronounced as to be a completely contrasting colour. Most of these plants have been developed from sports and have a tendency to revert to their original form; often this reversion appears on only one branch of a plant and can be easily removed.

Cultivars
'New Life' – can be double or single, red with white stripes.
'Mr Wren' – single, soft red with white edging.
'Gloriosa' – single, large, palest pink with red edging.
'Dr Tucker' – single, purple with red centre.
'Lizzie White' – double, white with pink edging.
'Shimmer' – double, apricot with white reverse.
'Will Rogers' – single, purple blotched with scarlet.
'Phlox Eye' – single, pink with red eye.
'Warley' – single, red with white eye.

Bird's-egg Cultivars
Bird's-egg cultivars are sometimes classified as a separate group; they are freckled or spotted and come only in shades of pink.

'Cooks Golden Bird's-egg' – coral, spotted with red, pale leaves.
'Mrs J. J. Knight' – single, pale pink spotted rose.
'Plenty' – double, large white spotted with lavender.

'Warley'

'Mr Wren'

'New Life'

'Cooks Golden Bird's egg'

'Gloriosa'

'Plenty'

'Lizzie White'

'Mrs J.J. Knight'

Zonal Pelargoniums – Variegated-Leaved

Variegated-leaved zonals are known to have been in cultivation for nearly 250 years, apparently arising from some natural sports of *P. inquinans*. In 1853, Peter Grieve, a gardener of Culford Hall, Bury St. Edmonds, in England, started to take an interest in producing hybrids from these sports. During the following fifteen years he developed a number of interesting cultivars which are still popular to this day, such as 'Lass o'Gowrie', 'Mrs Pollock' and 'Mr Henry Cox'. Since then, other growers have continued his work and produced the large number of cultivars available today.

These plants often have single or smaller flowers than those of other zonal pelargoniums but, as their main virtue lies in the decorative quality of their leaves, they can still provide a colourful display even when not flowering. They are useful for winter border and bedding plants in districts with temperate winter climates and are good in sheltered positions outside in cooler areas. They also make decorative indoor pot plants.

As the youngest shoots are the most colourful, it pays to encourage fresh growth by pinching out growing tips, it also promotes growth, and prevents them from becoming leggy. Do not overfeed them as this tends to destroy the colour intensity of the leaves.

Cultivars
Tri-colour, Leaves Green, White and Red
Lass o'Gowrie' – single, bright red.
'Mr Henry Cox' – single, rose pink.
'Mrs Pollock' – single, vermilion.
'Mrs Strang' – double, vermilion.
'Skies of Italy' – single, red.

Leaves Gold with Bronze Zone
'Ann Tilling' – single, deep salmon.
'Shannon' – single, salmon.
'Marechal Macmahon' – single, vermilion.
'Medallion' – single, salmon-red.
'Mrs Quilter' – single, pink.
'Golden Fleece' – double, rose.

Leaves Silver and Green
'Caroline Schmidt' – double, turkey red.
'Chelsea Gem' – double, pale pink.
'Petals' – single, deep pink.
'Mrs Mapping' – single, white.
'Ivory Snow' – double, white.
'Misty' – double, salmon, with white stems.
'Madame Salleron' – non-flowering.

Leaves Plain Gold
'Verona' – single, deep pink.
'Gold Crest' – single, orange-pink.
'Suffolk Gold' – single, scarlet.
'Robert Fish' – single, vermilion.
'Martins Gold' – single, pink.

Unusual Leaf
'A Happy Thought' – single, crimson; leaf centre ivory.
'Mangles' – single, red; butterfly marking on leaf.
'Distinction' – single, red; circular leaf with narrow dark ring.
'Tijuana Bronze' – single, salmon; bronze, green and brown leaf.
'Wantirna' – single, red; green leaf veined with white.

'Honey Fleece'

'Retah's Bronze'

'Henry Cox'

'Zig Zag' & 'Mangles'

'Shannon'

Ivy-Leaved Pelargoniums (ivy geraniums, *P. peltatum*)

In general, ivy-leaved pelargoniums are very hardy plants. They are not as prone to disease as the zonal pelargoniums, being almost totally resistant to rust, and will withstand poor soil, drought, mild frosts and some shade, though they will not flower in insufficient light.

P. peltatum is the only species in the pelargonium sub-genus Dibrachya. The name is from the Greek, *Peltatum*, meaning shield, and probably refers to the way that the leaf is held parallel to the stem, just as a shield is held away from the body. Its original habitat was Cape Province in South Africa. Little is known of its early cultivation or which other species were involved in the development of so many and different cultivars; it is thought that some species of the sub-genus Ciconium are the most probable partners.

The ivy-leaved pelargoniums' sprawling habit enables them to be used in many ways: for ground cover, for hanging over banks or walls, in rockeries or hanging baskets, even for climbing if given support.

The stems are thinner and longer between nodes than those of other pelargoniums, giving them a trailing habit. They become woody and rather brittle with age, breaking off easily at the node joints. Stems grow to about one metre (39 in) in length and do not branch freely although branching can be encouraged by pinching out the growing tips.

As the popular name suggests, the leaves resemble ivy leaves in shape, though are more succulent. They are often, though not always, zoned, and can also be variegated or veined.

The flowers can be single, semi-double or double though most commonly double. They have a habit of flowering copiously, resting for a short while and then flowering again, doing this several times during the year. Flower colours are generally whites, pinks and mauves though there are a few red varieties. Unlike zonals, the two top petals are larger than the lower ones.

shade, though will not flower in insufficient light.

Ivy-Leaved Pelargoniums – Single and Semi-Double

Single-flowered ivy-leaved pelargoniums are those on which the flowers have five petals. Semi-double flowers have more than five but less than eight petals. There are usually three to five flowers in a truss.

Cultivars
Single
'Sir A. Hort' – cerise.
'Valentine' – salmon, bronze marking on leaves.
'Red Ville de Paris' – orange-red.
'Rose Ville de Paris' – rose pink.
'Jeanne d'Arc' – large white and mauve, zoned leaves.

Semi-double
'Abel Carriere' – pale orchid-purple.
'Amethyst' – amethyst-mauve.
'Baden Powell' – white, feathered purple.
'La France' – mauve with white feathering of upper petals.
'Mexican Beauty' – dark red, paler reverse.
'Mrs Banks' – white and lilac.
'Apricot King' – apricot pink.
'Madame Crousse' – pale pink.
'Madame Mourrier' – salmon-rose, ruffled.
'Ruby Gibson' – salmon.
'Sir Percy Blakeney' – large, scarlet.
'Pink Carnation' – pink with darker pink fimbriated edging.
'Violet Beauty' – violet.

'Jeanne d'Arc'

Decorative effects

'Pink Carnation'

'Sir Percy Blakeney'

Ivy-Leaved Pelargoniums – Double

Double ivy-leaved pelargoniums have flowers with more than eight petals. They usually have five to eight flowers in a truss.

Cultivars

White

'Snowhite' ('Snowdrift', 'Snowflake') – white.

'The Duchess' ('Duchess of Valentois') – large, white, purple edge.

'Pearl Eclipse' – pearl white.

'Rouletta' – white with red edge.

Pink

'Apricot Queen' – soft apricot-pink, small, abundant flowers.

'Beauty of Jersey' – rose.

'Bridesmaid' – pale pink.

'Catalina' – deep orchid pink.

'El Gaucho' – large flower, deep pink.

'Flush Striped' – pale pink, striped rose.

'Galilee' – pink rosette, free-flowering.

'King Edward VII' – large flower, cerise pink.

'Leopard' – large flower, pink with crimson spots.

'Magna Carta' – salmon pink.

'Mrs H.J. Jones' – pink, edged carmine.

'Sybil Holmes' – pink, rose-like flowers.

Red

'Firedragon' – scarlet.

'Red Giroflee' – red pink rosette.

'Willy' – large flower, red.

'Wyck's Centurion' – large flower, soft red.

'Charles Monselet' – red-cerise.

'Monty' – orange-red.

'Simon Portas' – plum red.

Purples and Mauves

'Purple Giroflee' – purple rosette.

'New Purple' – deep purple.

'Blue Peter' – phlox mauve.

'Dr A. Chipault' – deep cerise-purple.

'Rigi' – large flower, deep cerise.

'Comptesse de Grey' – large flower, deep magenta.

'Joseph Warren' – purple.

'The Jester' – mauve-pink, free-flowering.

'Patricia' – pale mauve rosettes.

'Santa Paula' – lavender blue.

'The Jester'

'Rouletta'

'Leopard'

'Galilee'

'New Purple'

Ivy-Leaved Pelargoniums – Variegated and Miniature

There are only a few variegated cultivars of the ivy-leaved pelargoniums with a much more limited range of colours and variations than among the zonals. The majority have single flowers.

Miniature ivy-leaved cultivars are usually miniature in both leaf and flower size. They have short inter-nodal spaces leading to compact growth.

Variegated Leaves

'Aureum marginatum' – single, rose pink flower, yellow leaf.

'Crocodile' – single, deep rose flower, leaf veined with white.

'Golden Sallen' – single, salmon flower, yellow centre to leaf.

'L'Elegante' – single, white flower, leaves white and green with pink tinge when kept fairly dry.

'Sunset marble' or 'Wood's surprise' – single, pink flower, marbled green and white leaf.

'White Mesh' – single pink, veined leaf.

'Duke of Edinburgh' – small, rose pink flower, green and cream leaf.

'Elsi' – single red flower, green and cream leaf.

'Rose, Lady Lexington' – double pink flower, cream and green leaf.

'Valley Court' – double purple flower, leaf veined white.

'Pink Whitewood' – single pink flower, white stems and white zone on leaf.

'Beatrice Cottington' – double, purple rosette.

Miniatures

'Sugar Baby' – double, rose pink, free-flowering.

'Gay Baby' – single, mauve.

'Red Mini Cascade' – single, red, narrow petals.

'Rose Mini Cascade' – single, pink, narrow petals.

'Sugar Baby'

'Golden Sallen'

'White Mesh'

'Gay Baby'

'Crocodile'

'L'Elegante'

'Sunset marble' or 'Wood's Surprise'

'Red Mini Cascade'

Hybrid Ivy-Leaved Pelargoniums *P. peltatum* x *P. hortorum*

Hybrid ivies, as they are generally known, are a cross between ivy-leaved and zonal pelargoniums. They tend to look like zonals but have a drooping habit. These plants are very vigorous and free-flowering, and have the added advantage, inherited from the ivy-leaved pelargoniums, of being rust resistant.

Cultivars
'Antoine Crozy' – semi-double, scarlet.
'Picture' – semi-double, rose pink.
'Gretchen' – semi-double, red.
'Millfield Gem' – semi-double, pink with darker spots.
'King of Hearts' – double, light pink stippled red.
'Pink Alliance' – double, bright pink.
'Blue Spring' – double, bluish mauve.
'Achievement' – double, lavender pink.
'Pierre Crozy' – double, red.
'Schöne Schwarzwalderin' – double, dark pink.
'E. H. Trego' – double, bright orange.
'Madame Charmet' – double, scarlet.

'Antoine Crozy'

'Madame Charmet'

'Millfield Gem'

'Achievement'

56

Regal Pelargoniums *P.* x *domesticum*

Regal pelargoniums are half-hardy shrubs resulting from the hybridising of several pelargonium species from Cape Province and western areas of South Africa. *P. cucullatum* of the sub-genus Pelargonium is the principal ancestor. Each of the species involved in the development of the regal pelargoniums over the years has introduced a new colour element to the flower range – leading to the vast number of colour variations that are available today. *P. angulosum*, also of the sub-genus Pelargonium was the source of purple, *P. fulgidum* of the sub-genus Polyactium introduced red, and *P. grandiflorum* of the sub-genus Eumorpha added white to the colour range.

The name 'regal' dates from 1877, and seems to derive from the fact that many were developed in the royal greenhouses at Sandringham. In America they are known as 'Martha Washingtons'.

The plants are stiff, upright, compact shrubs about 40 to 60 cm (16 to 24 in) tall. Young succulent stems soon turn woody as they age.

The leaves are similar in most cultivars – roughly triangular, slightly lobed and with serrated edges they are often cupped or folded.

The flowers are carried in trusses of about five or six on shortish stems arising from the node joints. They are 4 to 5 cm (1½ to 2 in) wide with the petals either smooth or ruffled, and the two upper petals always larger than the three lower ones. Colours range from pure white to deep crimson, almost black, and through all shades of pink, red, mauve and orange. There are many different combinations of spots, edgings and petal reverses.

Flowering generally occurs only for a short period in late spring and early summer. If the dead flower heads are removed immediately after flowering there will often be another flowering period in late summer. The flowering time can also be extended by taking and establishing cuttings over a period of time.

Regals are very susceptible to green and white fly.

Regal Pelargoniums – Pink and White

Cultivars
'Alaska' – white with small purple veining in throat.
'Blizzard' – white with red blotch.
'Break of Day' – white with pale pink marking.
'Misty Mount' – white with dark blotch.
'Magpie' – small but free-flowering, white with deep purple blotch.
'Mrs James Rodgers' – white with pink band.
'Joan Morf' – white shaded rose pink.
'Hazel Ripple' – white with magenta blotch.
'The Doctor' – white with red splashes.
'White Swan' – pure white, large flower.
'White Chiffon' – pure white.
'Snow Fairy' – white with pink veining in throat.
'All My Love' – white mauve and crimson.

'Mrs James Rodgers'

'All My Love'

'Palm Beach'

Pink
'Andamooka' – pink with maroon blotch.
'Apple Blossom' – rose and white.
'Carisbrooke' – soft pink, frilled.
'Palm Beach' – rose pink, and ruffled
    large flower.
'Q2' – coral and maroon.
'Strawberry Sundae' – light pink, dark on
    upper petals.
'Moomba' – ruffled pink with deeper
    pink blotches.
'Vogue' – pink and red.
'Spring Song' – pink, large.
'Sunrise' – salmon pink with white
    throat.
'Tabriz' – salmon pink with dark blotch.
'Mariquita' – light and dark pink.

'Carisbrooke'

'Strawberry Sundae'

'Sunrise'

Regal Pelargoniums – Cultivars

Orange
'Orange Sal' – salmon-orange.
'Orange Splendour' – ruffled orange with pink reverse.
'Watermelon' – salmon with copper markings on upper petals.
'Goldie' – salmon with white base.
'744' – soft orange-salmon with dark splash.
'Dawn' – large flower, apricot.
'Music Man' – orange-red with crimson blotch.
'Autumn Festival' – orange-salmon, ruffled.
'Howards Orange' – orange with black flare on each petal.
'Tunias Perfecta' – orange-red, large and slightly ruffled.

'Amanda'

'Tunias Perfecta'

'Dawn'

Red
'Admiral Beresford' – rose and maroon with white centre.
'Amanda' – dark red.
'Antigua' – maroon with pink edging.
'Bonne Chance' – blood red.
'Conspicuous' – deep red with dark eye.
'Grand Slam' – red with dark splash.
'Vin Rouge' – dark wine-red.
'Opera House' – rose-magenta, ruffled, large flower.
'Princess of Wales' – frilly red, edged with white.
'Morweena' – dark maroon shaded to black.
'Bronze Velvet' – bronze-red with deeper blotches.
'Black Velvet' – deep crimson, almost black.
'South American Bronze' – maroon edged with white.
'Las Vegas' – bright red.
'Royal Ascot' – red with white stripes.
'Apollo' – deep blood-red.

'Vin Rouge'

'Pompeii'

'Lavender Grand Slam'

Regal Pelargoniums – Mauve and Purple

Cultivars

'Lavender Lace' – lavender and red, ruffled.

'Lilac Time' – deep lilac, ruffled.

'Lavender Grand Slam' – lavender with purple markings.

'Lavinia' – pale mauve blotched with deeper shade.

'Maid Marion' – frilly mauve.

'Lilac Emblem' – palest lilac, large and ruffled.

'Blue Bird' – blue-mauve.

'My Darling' – pale reddish-mauve, large.

'Parisienne' – mauve, upper petals marked with purple and black.

'Rembrandt' – deep purple and pale mauve edging.

'Empress of Russia' – purple with white edging.

'Ella' – purple, large.

'Pompeii' – dark brown-purple edged with white.

'Cezanne' – lavender-purple with dark markings.

'Intrigue' – almost black.

'Morfs Summer Storm' – two-tone purple.

'King Edmund' – large purple.

'Bonita' – purple and white.

'Rembrandt'

Pelargonium Species

There are over two hundred pelargonium species and it would be impracticable to mention them all here. The ones given below are those that are easily obtainable from specialist growers, and have some special quality that makes them interesting, either by virtue of their decorative form, their scent or because they are ancestors of the present garden hybrids.

A 'species' pelargonium is classified as one which grows true to seed and is, or has been, found growing in the wild.

These species are grouped according to their pelargonium sub-genus.

Eumorpha

P. alchemilloides found in several parts of South Africa.

Height 30 to 45 cm (12 to 18 in); hairy leaves; small pink flowers.

P. cotelydonis – from the island of St. Helena where it is called 'Old-man-live-for-ever'.

It is a spreading succulent about 30 cm (12 in) high; has very occasional small white flowers.

P. quinquelobatum – from Kenya and Ethiopia.

Prostrate shrub about 20 to 30 cm (8 to 12 in) in height; flowers, carried on long slender stems, are of an unusual greenish-pink colour.

P. tabulare – from Table Mountain, South Africa.

Height 15 to 30 cm (6 to 12 in); zoned leaf; small, cream coloured flowers.

Ligularia

P. hirtum – found on mountain slopes in western areas of South Africa.

Bushy shrub growing to 30 cm (12 in); carrot-like leaves; bright pink, purple-veined, flowers.

Pelargonium

P. cucullatum – from Capetown area.

Can grow up to 2 m (6 feet) high; principal parent of the regal pelargoniums; large crimson-mauve flowers.

P. denticulatum – from the banks of the Hex River South Africa.

Sixty to 90 cm (2 to 3 feet) in height; has very finely lobed and indented leaves that are almost fern-like in appearance; small, lilac flowers.

Other plants, sold as separate species, but almost certainly hybrids of *P. denticulatum* or at least very closely related, are *P. asperum* and *P. filicifolium*.

P. quercifolium – from damp areas in the hills of Cape Province.

Was introduced into Europe from South Africa in 1774 and has since been hybridised to form several 'oak-leaved geraniums' going under the various names of 'Endsleigh's prostrate oak', 'staghorn oak', 'royal oak', or 'Skelton's oak'. This low-growing prostrate plant is useful as a quick ground cover; it has purple flowers and dark-centred oak-shaped leaves and a height of about 60 cm (2 ft).

P. hispidum – shrub found in moist, shady situations in western districts of South Africa.

Height about 1 m (3 ft); large hairy leaves; small white flowers.

P. vitifolium – similar in habitat and appearance to *P. hispidum* except it has small purple flowers with a balm scent.

P. quercifolium

Polyactium

P. gibbosum – the 'gouty geranium', so called because of its swollen node joints; found growing in sandy soil around the coastline of South Africa.

Grows to about 1 m (3 ft) in height; has yellow, night-scented flowers.

P. triste – a tuberous rooted plant from gravelly slopes of south-western Cape Province.

Stemless, the leaf stalks, or petioles arise from the ground, and attain a height of about 30 to 40 cm (12 to 15 in); flowers are brown with yellow edges and night-scented.

Ciconium

P. acetosum – from Eastern Cape Province where it is found in stony soils and grassland.

Glossy-leaved shrub; 30 to 40 cm (12 to 15 in) high; salmon flowers.

P. frutetorum – one of the ancestors of the modern zonal pelargoniums, from Cape Province.

It reaches a height of 1 m (3 ft); bears small salmon pink flowers.

P. inquinans – from Cape Province.

The main parent of the 'zonals'; height 1 m (3 ft); red flowers though pink or white flowers have also been found in the wild.

Myrrhidium

P. myrrhifolium – common around Capetown area.

Thirty to 40 cm (12 to 15 in) high; flowers small, white veined with mauve fern-like leaves.

Cortusina

P. echinatum – a shrub found growing in the shade in parts of Namaqualand. It has short, prickly, succulent stems, the prickles are hardened stipules; height is 30 to 40 cm (12 to 15 in); flower colours vary between white, pink and purple.

Otidia

P. alternans – common on rocky slopes and hillsides of Karoo.

Branching succulent only 15 cm (6 in) high; small white flowers.

P. carnosum – grows in sandy soils, in semi-desert vegetation in south-west Cape Province.

Has tuberous roots and thick succulent stem; carrot-like leaves; small white flowers; requires very little water.

P. polycephalum – grows in sandy soil in western areas of South Africa.

A hairy-leaved succulent about 30 to 40 cm (12 to 15 in) high; small pink flowers.

P. frutotorum

'*P. polycephalum* 'Blandfordianum'   'Blandfordianum alba'

Scented-Leaved Pelargonium Species

Scented pelargoniums have been grown in herb gardens for the past three hundred years and much cross-pollination has taken place – consequently it is often hard to distinguish which are true species and which are hybrids. The following lists are of true species with their hybrid relations also mentioned.

Whatever their ancestry, scented pelargoniums are very useful plants. They can be used as ground cover or edging plants, and in pots for hanging baskets, providing not only scent, when crushed or brushed against, but also many useful flavours for culinary purposes. They vary greatly in size, appearance and growing habits. However, though the flowers are often small and undistinguished they are usually produced in copious numbers.

While some of the scents attributed to these plants are obvious and definite, such as the peppermint scent of *P. tomentosum* or the lemon scent of *P. crispum*, others are very vague and indicate a vivid display of imagination on the part of the namer.

P. asperum – pine scented.
Height 60 cm (24 in); bushy; lilac flowers; rough grey-green leaves. Possibly a hybrid between *P. denticulatum* and *P. radens*.

P. capitatum – rose scented – sometimes called 'Attar of roses'.
Height 60 cm (24 in); has a hairy leaf; rose-purple flowers. A variegated type is called 'Both's snowflake'.

P. crispum – lemon scented.
Height 90 cm (35 in); shrubby, upright plant; small crinkled leaves; mauve flowers. Sometimes called 'the fingerbowl geranium' as the leaves, in times past, were floated in fingerbowls for their fragrance. A variegated type called 'Prince Rupert' is often used in floral art work. Other hybrid plants known for their lemon scent are: 'Martin's Citrus', 'Lemon Fancy', 'Lethie', 'Little Gem' and 'Mabel Grey' – the latter having the strongest scent.

P. citriodorum – orange scented – often called 'Prince of Orange'.
Height 60 cm (24 in); mauve flowers; probably a hybrid. Another similar variety is called 'Orange Nectar'.

P. fragrans (or *fragrantissimum*) – nutmeg or spice scented.
Height 60 cm (24 in); small grey-green leaves; white flowers; rounded, compact plant. There is also a variegated form with mauve flowers.

P. crispum

'Mabel Gray'

P. graveolens – variously described in different publications as lemon, orange or rose scented; it remains with the inhaler to decide.

Height 1 m (3 ft); deeply cut, five-lobed leaves of grey-green; small flowers are pink spotted with purple. Grown commercially in some countries for the distillation of 'geranol', a substance used in the perfume industry. A variegated cultivar is called 'Lady Plymouth'.

P. grossulariodes – coconut scented.

Height 15 cm (6 in); creeping habit, stems reaching 50 cm (20 in) in length; small leaves; purple flowers; moist, shady habitat preferred. Another coconut scented type is called 'Upright Coconut', this has small yellow flowers and deeply lobed leaves.

P. nervosum – lime scented.

Height 30 to 40 cm (12 to 16 in); small crinkled leaves; lavender flowers.

P. odoratissimum – apple scented.

Height 20 to 30 cm (8 to 12 in); sprawling plant; small white flowers. In the wild grows as undergrowth in forest areas of South Africa.

P. scabrum – apricot scented.

Height 40 to 60 cm (16 to 24 in); the leaf is three-lobed, harsh and hairy; flowers are white with purple markings. Another plant with scarlet flowers and lower growth, sold as 'Apricot Scented' is probably a hybrid.

P. tomentosum – peppermint scented.

Height 40 cm (16 in); large, velvety, light green leaves; small white flowers; quick ground cover. A hybrid called 'Joy Lucille' is also peppermint scented.

Other hybrids, available from specialist growers, claim the following scents: 'Lady Scarborough' (strawberry), 'Clorinda' (eucalyptus), 'Pretty Polly' (almond), *P. torento* (ginger), 'Robers Lemon-rose', 'Clare's Cascade' (apple-mint), as well as many others which are just listed as 'Cinnamon scented', 'Chocolate scented', 'Camphor-rose' or 'Citronella'.

P. nervosum

'Clorinda'

'White Orbit'

F.1 Hybrids

There are now many different F.1 hybrid seeds (seeds that grow true to type) being produced in both Europe and America – mainly for commercial pot plant growers. Their advantages to commercial growers are obvious: it is much easier to grow large numbers of pot and bedding plants from seed than to have to maintain large plantations from which to obtain a sufficiency of cuttings for the modern, super-market type of plant selling. For this reason large plant centres now seem to supply more seed-grown plants than cutting-grown cultivars. Seed-grown plants can be used both as potplants and as garden bedding plants, and they appear to flower well over a longer period than the cutting-grown plants.

Until recently their main disadvantage used to be that they were only single flowering zonal pelargoniums with a limited colour range. Now, however, each year brings new and better varieties and these will, no doubt, soon be superceded by others.

There are now many types represented in the growing list of available seeds: dwarf, stellar, speckled, ivy-leaved, floribunda and some developed particularly for hanging baskets. F.2. hybrids (second cross) are also being developed.

A brief list of these varieties can usefully be divided into types and series – each series containing several colour variations, often with individual names.

Standard types
'Sprinter' series.
'Carefree' series.
'Orbit' series.
'Gala' series.
'Century' series.
Some well known individual standard types are:
'Cherry glow'
'Adrette'
'Double Scarlet Marathon'
'Red Elite'
'Merlin'
'Sundance orange'.

Multi flora or Floribunda types
'Diamond' series.
'Pinto' series.

Dwarf types
'Gremlin' series.
'Playboy' series.
'Video' series.

Stellar types
'Stardust' series.

Basket types
'Fountain' series.
'Breakaway' series.

Ivy-leaved types
'Summer showers'

Unusual types
'Bright eyes', red with white eye.
'Speckles', with streaks and spots.
'Eyes right', dark eye.

F.2. hybrids
'Fleuriste' series.
'Paint Box' series.
' Sprite' series.

Oddments – Unique, Angel and Miniature Regal Pelargoniums

There are a number of plants developed from early hybridising experiments that have persisted. For instance, the groups called Uniques are mentioned in catalogues dating back to the early nineteenth century. They are thought to have been developed in part from the species *P. fulgidum*. There are others, sometimes called 'Old Fashioned Pelargoniums' or 'Garden Pelargoniums' –

'Merlin'

also of indeterminate ancestry – which, in districts with mild climates, are much used to cover problem areas or unsightly corners, as they require little attention, yet produce an abundance of flowers. Both of these types resemble the regal pelargoniums in leaf form although the flowers are considerably smaller.

Cultivars
'Pink or Rose Unique' – deep pink with darker markings.
'Rollinsons Unique' – magenta and red.
'Scarlet Unique' – red with darker markings.
'Purple Unique' – purple with darker markings.
'Scarlet Pet' – turkey red veined with black.
'Shrubland Pet' – rose veined with black.
'Madame Nonin' – deep pink with lighter pink centre and edge.
'Charles E. Pearson' – dark red.
'Claret Rock' – red and pink.
'Pink Feather' – white feathered with pink.
'Stoneleigh' – rose with pale centre.

Another group, developed in the mid-1930s by Mr Langley-Smith of London, is the Angel Pelargoniums. They rarely exceed 25 cm (10 in) in height and have small crinkled leaves similar to *P. crispum*, from which they may be in some part derived. Their flowers are quite large in comparison to the size of the plant, and are borne freely for several months. They are delightful, small, pot plants.

Though Angel Pelargoniums are sometimes listed as Miniature Regals, this is not strictly correct, there is a small group of plants that are truly miniature versions of that plant, having identical, though smaller, leaves.

Cultivars
'Catford Belle' – rose-purple.
'Gosbeck' – pale lavender.
'Hemingstone' – lavender veined with magenta.
'Madam Layal' – dark plum outlined white.
'Manx Maid' – purple with pink base.
'Mrs G.H. Smith' – white with pink markings.
'Rose Bengal' – rose-purple with paler edges.
'Sancho Panza' – purple and white.
'Black knight' – dark crimson with paler edging.
'Valenza' – royal purple and white.
'Fred Thomas' – deep maroon with purple edged. Miniature Regal.

P. x *blandfordianum* (Clifford) is sometimes listed with species plants, but is in fact a primary hybrid. It is known to have been raised in 1805 in the glasshouses of the Marquis of Blandford – hence the name – and is thought to be a cross between *P. graveolens* and *P. odoratissimum* though this is by no means certain. They have seven-lobed, aromatic leaves and are free-flowering. There are two varieties: *P.* x *b.* var. *alba* and *P.* x *b.* var. *rosea* bearing white and pink flowers respectively.

'Mrs G.H. Smith'

'Black Knight'

'Rose Unique'

'Catford Belle'

Video – hybrid seedling (green-white-pink)

Glossary

Actinomorphic	(of a flower) identical when cut in any vertical plane through the centre.
Awn	stiff bristle at the top of the seed sheath.
Axis	central column.
Calyx	outer ring of the parts of a flower, composed of **sepals**, usually green but sometimes coloured.
Carpel	modified leaf in the female part of the flower **pistil**, which produces the ovule.
Cordate	heart-shaped.
Cultivar	a named variety of a cultivated plant.
Epidermis	outer layer of the stem or leaf.
Family	group of allied genera of plants.
Genus, plural genera	group of closely related plants, subordinate to **family**, having common structural characteristics.
Hybrid	the result of cross fertilising any two plants; a primary hybrid or first cross is the result of cross fertilising plants of two different species.
Inflorescence	collective flower, i.e. cluster of flowers forming one bloom.
Internode	stem between two leaf-joints or nodes.
Lobes	small separate cavities in a fruit or seed pod.
Locules	part of a petal or leaf which is divided from the rest by a deep indentation of the margin.
Mutant	plant with inheritable genetic change which has resulted from sudden variation in the hereditary material of the cell.
Naturalised	plant which has adopted a new country where it grows and multiplies in the wild.
Nectar-spur	nectar-producing tube attached to flower stem (**pedicel**).
Node	point at which the leaf stalk (**petiole**) grows from the stem.
Ovule	rudimentary seed or female germ-cell of seed-plants.
Palmate	palm-shaped – having lobes like spread fingers.
Panicle	inflorescence made up of a series of clusters of flowers.

Pedicel	flower stalk.
Peduncle	the stalk of a flower, fruit, or cluster, especially the main stalk bearing a solitary flower or subordinate stalks.
Petiole	leaf stalk.
Pistil	female (seed bearing) part of a flower.
Rotate	round-shaped.
Sepals	leaves of the **calyx**, surrounding the bud.
Simple	leaf undivided.
Species	group of plants, subordinate to a genus, that differs in a number of significant details and usually reproduces consistently true from seed.
Sport	plant or part of a plant which deviates suddenly or strikingly from normal type.
Stipule	leafy growth at base of leaf stalk.
Succulent	thick or fleshy leaves or stems.
Truss	cluster of flowers.
Variegation	where the leaf is marked with regular or irregular patches of different colour.
Variety	subordinate plant of a particular species differing morphologically in only one or two botanically minor details such as flower colour or height. They often interbreed freely.
Veining	where the veins of a petal or leaf are easily distinguishable due to a difference in colour.
Umbel	flower cluster in which the flower stalks (**pedicels**) spring from a common centre on the end of the flower stem (**peduncle**).
Zygomorphic	flower divisible into similar halves only on one plane.

Appendix I

Uses in Floral Art

Though not often thought of as 'floral-art' flowers, pelargoniums do keep very well in water – they will last for about two weeks, if picked early in their development.

As the flowers in each inflorescence open from the centre outwards, the centre of the bloom has a tendency to die before the whole head is open. If the dying centre flowers are removed with tweezers, or carefully nipped out with the fingers, the developing flowers will usually cover the empty space, prolonging the use of the bloom.

Almost any pelargonium cultivars can be used, but double flowers tend to last better, particularly the tightly double 'rosebud' cultivars. The latter are especially useful for buttonholes and smaller arrangements.

The foliage of pelargoniums, with its great variety of shapes and colours, is of even more use to the floral artist than the flowers. From the large plain green leaves of the zonal pelargoniums, to the trailing branches of the ivy-leaved pelargoniums, with or without strong zonal markings, they offer many variations in structure and size. Many of the variegated and coloured leaf varieties provide splashes of colour when flowers are in short supply, or add touches of light to foliage arrangements.

Cultivars and colours available are listed on pages 32-60, but any gardener growing plants for a floral artist should also consider the scented cultivars and species plants, particularly *P. tomentosum* with its large, furry, soft-green leaves, *P. crispum* var. 'Prince Rupert' which bears long sprays of small crinkled leaves with cream edging, or 'Lady Plymouth' the variegated cultivar of *P. graveolens* with its deeply cut, grey-green leaves.

As can be seen in the photograph containing the bright red flowers, developing seed heads can also be used to good effect.

Leaves being used in any arrangement will benefit from an overnight soaking before use, but flowers are best picked early on the morning that they will be required, and placed straight into water.

Appendix II

Uses of Scented Pelargonium Leaves

Pot Pourri
Mixed leaves from any of the scented pelargonium cultivars can be used for pot pourri. Dry well by spreading leaves on sheets of paper in an airy room or in an airing cupboard that is not too hot. Mix dried leaves with paper-dry rose petals, lavender heads, etc. Sprinkle with a mixture of 2 oz (0.07 ml) table salt, 2 oz (0.07 ml) borax powder and ¼ oz (0.05 ml) ground cinnamon. Cover and stir daily for two or three weeks. Placed in a bowl, and turned each day, this pot pourri will impart a delicate perfume to a room for about one year; kept in a lidded glass jar, and opened daily for a short time, it will retain its perfume for several years.

Uses in Cooking
Apple scented (*P. odoratissimum*) leaves can be added to apple jelly in the last few minutes of cooking then removed. Inserted in the centre of baked apples with sugar and butter they are edible when cooked. In both cases they intensify the apple flavour.

Nutmeg scented (*P. fragrans*) leaves add flavour to chicken stews and casseroles.

Lemon scented (*P. crispum*) leaves added to rice puddings or baked custards give a delicate lemon flavour. Variously described in different publications as lemon, orange or rose scented, it remains with the inhaler to decide.

Rose scented (*P. capitatum* or *P. graveolens*) can be placed in the bottom of a cake tin before baking a sponge cake.

Peppermint scented (*P. tomentosum*) leaves can be used wherever a peppermint flavour is desired. The Greeks traditionally placed a fresh leaf in jars of setting apple jelly to decorate them and to give a hint of peppermint flavour.

Appendix III

Geranium and Pelargonium Societies

Australian Geranium Society	Honorary Secretary: Mrs G. Perry 118 Thorney Road Fairfield West, NSW 2165
South African Pelargonium & Geranium Society	PO Box 55342 Northlands Johannesburg 2116 South Africa
The British Pelargonium and Geranium Society	23 Beech Crescent Kidlington Oxford OX5 1DW United Kingdom
Auckland Carnation, Gerbera & Geranium Society	2091 Great North Road Avondale Auckland
International Geranium Society	5861 Walnut Drive Eureka California 95501 USA

Appendix IV

Some Suggested Further Reading

Bagust, H. — 1968 *Miniature Geraniums*, John Gifford, London.

Bennett, Monica — 1972 *Geraniums, the Successful Growers Guide*, Bartholomew, Edinburgh.

Clifford, Derek — 1958 (several later editions) *Pelargoniums, Including the Popular 'Geranium'*, Blandford Press, London.

Farthing, J. G. — 1981 *Geraniums from Seed*, (Growers Guide No. 25) Grower Books, London.

Keys, Hazel — 1985 *Pelargoniums* (Wisley handbook series). The Royal Horticultural Society, Vincent Square, London.

Llewellyn, Hudson & Morrison — 1982 *Geraniums & Pelargoniums*, Kangaroo Press, Australia.

Mastalerz, J. W. and Holcomb, E. J. — 1982 *Geraniums III*, (research papers from Pennsylvania State University) Pennsylvania Flower Growers, 102 Tyson Building, University Park, PA 16802, USA.

Schultz, P. — 1965 *All About Geraniums*, Doubleday & Co., New York.

Webb, William, J. — 1984 *The Pelargonium Family*, Croom Helm, London

Witham Fogg, H. G. — 1964 *Geraniums and Pelargoniums*, John Gifford, London.

Van der Walt, Dr J. J. — 1977 *Pelargoniums of Southern Africa*, E. Ward-Hilhorst, Purnell, South Africa.

Yeo, Peter — 1985 *Hardy Geraniums*, Croom Helm, London.

Appendix V

SOURCES OF SUPPLY

PELARGONIUM PLANTS

Beckwood Nurseries, New Inn Road, Beckley, Near Oxford, OX3 9SS.

Clifton Geranium Nurseries, Cherry Orchard Road, Whyke, Chichester, Sussex, PO19 2BX.

Fibrex Nurseries, Honeybourne Road, Pebworth, Near Stratford-on-Avon, CV37 8XT.

D. Gamble and Sons, Highfield Nurseries, Longford, Derbyshire, DE6 3DT.

Grimston Park Nurseries, Tadcaster, North Yorkshire, LS24 9DB.

Monica Bennett, Cypress Nursery, Powke Lane, Blackheath, Birmingham.

Redvale Nurseries, St Tudy, Bodmin, Cornwall, PL30 3PX.

Thorp's Nurseries, 257 Finchhampstead Rd, Wokingham, Berkshire, RG11 3JT.

Vernon Geranium Nursery, Cuddington Way, Cheam, Sutton, Surrey, SM2 7JB.

SEED SUPPLIERS

Dobies Seeds, PO Box 90, Paignton, Devon, TQ3, 1XY.

Suttons Seeds, Hele Road, Torquay, Devon, TQ2 7QJ.

Thompson and Morgan, London Road,
Ipswich, Suffolk, IP2 OBA.

Unwins Seeds, Impington Lane, Histon,
Cambridge, CB4 4LE.

GERANIUMS AND ERODIUMS
Bressingham Gardens, Diss, Norfolk,
IP22 2AB.

Margery Fish Nursery, East Lambrook Manor,
South Petherton, Somerset, TA13 5HL.

Holden Clough Nursery, Holden,
Bolton-by-Bowland,
Clitheroe, Lancashire, BB7 4PF.

Oland Plants, Sawley Nursery, Risplith, Ripon,
North Yorkshire, NG4 3EW.

W.E. Th. Ingwersen Ltd., Birch Farm Nursery,
Gravetye, East Grinstead, West Sussex,
RH19 4LE.

Unusual Plants, White Barn House,
Elmstead Market,
Colchester, Essex, CO7 7DB.